POEMS AND TRANSLATIONS OF HĬ-LÖ

The Poems and Translations of Hĭ-Lö

JOHN PECK

CARCANET

First published in 1991 by
Carcanet Press Limited
208-212 Corn Exchange Buildings
Manchester M4 3BQ

Copyright © 1991 John Peck
All rights reserved

British Library Cataloguing in Publication Data
Peck, John
  Poems and translations of Hi-Lo.
  I. Title
  821.914

ISBN 0 85635 870 3

The publisher acknowledges the financial assistance
of the Arts Council of Great Britain

Set in 10pt Palatino by Bryan Williamson, Darwen
Printed and bound in England by SRP Ltd, Exeter

Contents

Acknowledgements	8
Editor's Preface	11
Four Ancient Poems	13
January Inventory	14
Joys of the Rich	16
Ditty for Mayor Fu of Freiburg im Breisgau	18
Rhyme Prose One	20
A Hero's Life	21
Rhyme Prose Two	22
Forged Heart Blade	24
En Avant de nos jours	25
Tally Stick	26
Sotheby Parke Bernet Renga (muted)	27
A Sash for Wu Yün	29
The Death of Yuri Andropov	34
Rhyme Prose Three: Chapter of the Nine Rocks	35
"Vega over the rim of the Val Verzasca"	37
Clam Shell with Hunting Scene	38
"Fifteen stars fence polar fire..."	40
Bird Garden	41
Novissima Sinica	44
Round Trip Chanties	45
Sorting Straws	46
"And what do they do..."	49
Hazelnut	50
Fantasia for Du Bellay	51
Osip Mandelshtam in the Grisons	52
Wind Under Sash, Val Ferret	54
Rhyme Prose Four	55
Fleurs d'essence	57
Seventh Moon	58
Spring Housecleaning	63
Rhyme Prose Five	64
Colgan over Cogitosus, or Kan Pao Prosimetrics	65
Anti-dithyrambics	68
Reading Western Masters	69
A Gross of Poems Linked in the Mixed Manner	70
Rhyme Prose Six	92

Hill Country Ballad	94
The Cells at Tun-huang	95
Tail of the Magpie	96

•

Folksong II.xii of the Classic Anthology	99
Honan Folksong	99
from Folksong I.ix of the Greater Odes, Classic Anthology	100
"Where the cypresses of Ox Mountain", Mencius	100
Single Seal Quodlibets	101
Pavanne before the Winter Campaign	102
Two and Three Seal Medley	103
Chou Medley	103
Age of Gold	105
Barometric Reading Incorporating Single Graphs	105
Western Palace Rhapsodies	106
"Writing alters...", Liu Xie	107
Lament in Wet Spring, Li Ho	107
Dawn in Shih-Cheng, Li Ho	108
from Twenty-three Poems about Horses, Li Ho	108
"Cold Mountain writes you this", Han-shan	109
"'For whom did you strip off your finery?'", Tung-Shan Liang-chieh	110
Weeping for Ying Yao, Wang Wei	110
Sent to Yü Te Fu on His Receiving a Commission..., Tsung Ch'en	111
"Emptiness at ease...", Wang Yang-ming	112
The Proem (opening), Parmenides	113
Excerpts, Homer and Callimachus	113
Orphic Fragment	114
Epitaph for Albert Bertschy	114
Christian epigram, Palatine Anthology L.59	115
from Poem on Divine Providence, Orientius, early fifth century	115
"Inten bec", anonymous Irish, ninth century	116
"What enwombed the marrow...", Walahfrid Strabo	116
Travellers to Broceliande	117
On an Almond Tree in Hungary, Janus Pannonius	118
Gouty Brigit: Epigram I.284, Janus Pannonius	119
My Country Weeps: 1636, Andreas Gryphius	120
Goethemathy	121
The Course of Life, Friedrich Hölderlin	123
from The Tombs, Ugo Foscolo	124

from The Graces, Ugo Foscolo 125
Rawlinson Two-Step (anonymous English, with "The Public
    Slanderers", Gottfried Keller) 125
Venus de Milo, Gottfried Keller 127
"Quand elle viendra..." Oscar V. de L. Milosz 127
Bridge on the Rhine, Oscar V. de L. Milosz 128
Hidden Name, Victor Segalen 129
from Contemplation, Victor Segalen 130
"Solang du Selbstgeworfenes fängst...", R.M. Rilke 130
A cento *from* Valais Quatrains, R.M. Rilke 131
Snow, Robert Walser 132
Evening on Reichenau, Martin Heidegger 133
Postcard from the Engadine, Kurt Tucholsky 133
Underworld North of Lugano, Rudolf Borchardt 134
"Gehölz...", Peter Huchel 136
Po-Chü-I, Peter Huchel 137
Resurrection, Peter Huchel 138
"In der Verwitterung alter", Peter Huchel 138
Novgorod: Coming of the Saints, Johannes Bobrowski 139
Assisi, Paul Celan 140
On Reading a Recent Greek Poet (*Buckow Elegies*), Bertolt Brecht 141
Li Po, Albin Zollinger 141
Mother of Kindnesses, Erika Burkart 142
Between Nights, Tudor Arghezi 142
Downpressings, Ion Barbu 143
Century, Ion Barbu 143
To the Workers in Spain, Vladimír Holan 144
September 1938. IV, Vladimír Holan 144
May 1945, Vladimír Holan 145
Vintage, Vítězslav Nezval 147
Slaughterhouse, Vítězslav Nezval 147
Roman Lines, Óndra Lysohorsky 148
House, Óndra Lysohorsky 149
Yu-Vu Songs of the Na-khi 150

Notes 155

Acknowledgements

Some of these poems have appeared in *Agenda, Antaeus, Delos, Ironwood, PN Review, Salmagundi,* and *TriQuarterly,* as well as in *The Noble Traveller: O.V. de L. Milosz,* ed. Christopher Bamford. Thanks are due to their editors as well as to the following persons: Elizabeth Burr for her support, Christoph Frey and Peter Viereck (for their information on Borchardt), Lucy Lo (for advice on Lǐ Hö), Christopher Middleton in his essays on Zurich Dada, David Oswald (for advice on Borchardt and Tucholsky), and Valerie Hylton, William Lafleur, Bruce and Gaby Lawder, the late Paul McNeil, William Mullen, Keith Parker, and Mark Temmer, for assorted *données.* Thanks also to the John Simon Guggenheim Memorial Foundation, for support during a period when a few of these poems came into the editor's hands.

Copyright Permissions

Tudor Arghezi, "Întra Două Nopți", *Versuri I,* © 1980, Cartea Romanesca, Bucharest

Ion Barbu, "Încleștări" and "Secol", *Nadir Latent,* © 1985, Editura Minerva, Bucharest

Johannes Bobrowski, "Nowgorod (Ankunft der Heiligen)", *Wetterzeichen: Gedichte,* © 1966, Union Verlag (VOB), Berlin

Rudolf Borchardt, "Unterwelt hinter Lugano", *Gesammelte Werke in Einzelbänden, Gedichte* II / *Ubertragungen* II, © 1985, Klett-Cotta, Stuttgart

Bertolt Brecht, "Bei der Lektüre eines spätgriechischen Dichters", *Werke* 12: *Gedichte* 2, © 1988, Aufbau Verlag, Berlin / Weimar and Suhrkamp Verlag, Frankfurt am Main; and the Brecht Estate

Erika Burkart, "Holdermutter", *Ich Lebe: Gedichte,* © 1964, Artemis Verlag, Zürich / Stuttgart; permission of the author

Paul Celan, "Assisi", *Von Schwelle zu Schwelle,* © 1955, Deutsche Verlags-Anstalt GmbH, Stuttgart

Martin Heidegger, "Abendgang auf der Reichenau", *Gesamtausgabe* I: 13, © 1983, Vittorio Klostermann GmbH, Frankfurt am Main. Heidegger's version of lines from the *Tao Te Ching* appears in his letter to Paul Shih-yi Hsiao, "Heidegger and Our Translation of the *Tao Te Ching*", *Heidegger and Asian Thought*, © 1987, ed. Graham Parkes, University of Hawaii

Vladimír Holan, "Setkáni V", "Španělským dělníkům", "Září 1938 IV: Noc z Iliady", and "Květen 1945", *Sebrané spisy* II: *Ale je hudba*, © 1968, Vydal Odeon, Prague; *Vladimír Holan: nočni hlídka srdce*, © 1963 Československy Spisovatel, Prague; *Tobě*, © 1985 [1947], Vydal Odeon, Prague; and the Holan Estate

Peter Huchel, "Pe-Lo-Thien", "Gehölz...", and "In der Verwitterung alter", *Gesammelte Werke* I: *Die Gedichte*, © 1984, Suhrkamp Verlag, Frankfurt am Main

Óndra Łysohorsky, "Römische Zeilen" and "Das Haus", *Danksagung*, © 1961, Insel Verlag, Leipzig

Oscar V. de L. Milosz, "Quand elle viendra..." and "Le Pont sur le Rhin", *Œuvres complètes: Poésies* I & II, © 1960, Éditions André Silvaire, Paris; © John Peck

Vítězslav Nezval, "Kentauři" (*Česky Balady*) and "Jatky" (*Pět Minut za Mestem*, 1939) in *Dílo* VIII, © 1954, and "Vinobrani" (*Absolutní hrobař*, 1937), in *Dílo* XI, © 1958, Československy Spisovatel, Prague

R.M. Rilke, "Solang du Selbstgeworfenes fängst, ist alles" and "Les Quatrains Valaisans", *Sämtliche Werke* II, © 1986, Insel Verlag, Frankfurt am Main

Kurt Tucholsky, "Kartengruss aus dem Engadin", *Gesemmalte Werke* II, © 1960, Rowohlt Verlag GmbH, Reinbek bei Hamburg

Robert Walser, "Schnee", *Sämtliche Werke in Einzelausgaben* XIII: *Die Gedichte*, © 1986, Suhrkamp Verlag, Zürich / Frankfurt am Main

Albin Zollinger, "Li-Tai-Pe", *Werke* 4: *Gedichte*, © 1983, Artemis Verlag, Zürich / München

*Stopped by a woman
        at the gate of a strange town,
I implored, "Let me pass, I'm pacing
just to keep going back and forth, because
I'm afraid of the dark like anyone else".
And she said to me,
"But there is the lamp, I left it burning"!*

– Vladimír Holan, "Encounter V"
  c. 1943-48

Preface

The writer and translator of these poems is a Chinese intern in psychosomatics who worked in Zurich during the 1980s and used his writing as a way of adapting to the West. He returned to China just before the Eastern European revolutions of 1989. The anomaly of a Swiss situation was eased for him by the historical resemblance it bore to the ministate administered by Guan Zhong, compiler of the *Guanzi* and a model for Confucius, which had to exercise cleverness in order to survive among more powerful neighbours to the north and south. Both the anomaly and the cleverness, in a formerly peasant culture turned affluent beyond even its folktale dreams of wealth, were further eased by his taking stock of Gottfried Keller's prophecy that there would come a day when "a great deal of money will find its way to our country which we have neither earned nor saved, and then truly the Devil will get his teeth into our necks, and the fabric and dyes in our flag will begin to mean something".

To the voluminous and inconclusive speculations in the West about the significance of the East, Hī-Lö's efforts do not pertain, unless as a belwether trotting alongside Dr John Wu's contention that any synthesis of these opposites would take place first in the West. Hī-Lö's own notes are rather sceptical about any such synthesis, however. Across one folder he scrawled, "It does not add up" – a folder containing oriental lyrics and epigrams by Peter Huchel and Johannes Bobrowski, but also the ethically questionable Heidegger's Lao Tzu,* and quatrains by the political theorist Carl Schmitt, whose ambiguous career during the Third Reich does not leave one thrilling to his testimony that "a holy man from the East led me through the saving gates".†

Since Hī-Lö's parentage was mixed (a Japanese father from the Manchurian invasion, with an American missionary as the maternal grandfather), it comes as no surprise that he did not wince at the contortions into which he bent oriental traditions, or at his adaptations of Western practices, or at his resort to languages of which he had no thorough knowledge in order to make music for which he could supply no living context. Hī-Lö remained the child of his age in this, that he followed

---

* "Ethically questionable": Heidegger himself treated the "questionable" as a pre-eminent category which included the unpleasant extreme of *Erschütterung*. The strenuous conversation among nations which he urged but for which he receives little credit in the current questioning of his record was of course valued by Hī-Lö, who counted Heidegger, in spite of his errors, as its most reflective. recent spokesman.
† The line quoted from Carl Schmitt concludes his post-war poem, "Song of the Sexagenarian".

the pack into this peculiar territory and pitched his tent in their desert. From beneath its flaps his shepherd songs dispersed among the circumambient ditties of Berber herdsmen, Siberian shamans, Zuñi initiates, and Aztec priests.

David Gascoyne has observed that poets writing in English still compose homages to their cultural predecessors, as a form of iconography carrying forward the impulses of Eliot and Pound in what Mr Gascoyne construes as a salvage operation. Pound, however, argued that "shoring" things was one matter and "shelving" them quite another, the shelf providing no salvage post but rather a stage for new alignments. While Hī-Lö was no theorist, his sense of renovation (witness the fragment from Liu Xie) assumes the force of that distinction, and his homages have as their reverse side a frequent impulse to satire. He saw no allure in Western mystifications of silence, whether from motives of experiment or historical guilt. Perhaps like renovation in his tradition, silence is the equilibrium of a steady hum, just as presentation in his version of an archaic source, is statement. The renovation he most valued in twentieth-century European poetry flew no flag at the head of an advancing column, for instance as with Jiří Kolář's orientalizing "Ars Poetica of Master Sun". It was the attempt at a new Christian metaphysics in the late prose poems of Oscar Milosz, in a statement of findings that assumed the priority of changes other than those of style, and which Hī-Lö knew lay well beyond the translatable reach of his compatriots. "This elixir will suffer no rebottling", he scribbled next to verse 81 in *Les Arcanes* (the translation is by Czesław Miłosz): "Here, in this tool bag, O King of toilers, you will find the cross, the scepter and the crown of the world. But I must tell you once more how the ancient King became blind".

After the democracy movement died in Tien An Men Square, Hī-Lö returned to practise medicine. Scattered notes indicate his awareness that the manuscript he left behind elegized a European era which had recoiled into memorials and cenotaphs *pour mieux sauter*, whether with mindfulness or amnesia it remains to be seen. The farewell taped to his bicycle combines part of Tristan Tzara's "Sagacity Dance Number Two", written in Zurich, with a stanza of his own: "Thickening fog from unexpected fans / impassive high-voltage arc that fastens / corridors spine of roofs and smoke / degree of wind that rips the washing", and then, "A shaken excellence / T-squared from Homer by Pythagoras / and sprocketed to this circle / whirling below? / 'Of foot, of fighting, of mind'."

Four Ancient Poems

Between the life mask of Jefferson
    nearly stifling him
and the suicide of Forrestal
slides a breath held indefinitely
    and a face evaporating to phantoms.

Ballads dissolve to utterance
in the browns of rivers, *megalopolitans*,
in loam and bran chaff and oxides of alloys
scampering through the slow strobe of sun.

My horse drank from little caves in the Wall.
    For miles, bones littering moonlight.
And who will judge the guilty? Thousands
stipple the field, naked stubble, and my mount
    takes her way, treading the shadow's edge.

Between utterance and river
stands, it seems, a lone speaker
    tided by multitudes
streaming from then through now, streaming.

January Inventory

        Man hath made marvels,
        twin stone towers, and spotlights
        bringing them snow, ranked jaws
        spitting radiance
        at the imperial profile

Preserved to two hundred so as to bear visions in the night
of flurrying blood and tumbling towers, and then grief,
and then the coffin of pale stone back to Blaye, that pall
sleeving in silk three hearts out of thirteen, Charlemagne
who ran stumbling beneath the trees "does not want to go forth".

        And sword over the stone lap
        of the emperor. And cup
        where a snake deposited its ring,
        a gold ring for him,
        to paint the field of his gaze, widest
        field of instruction, hours
        of gold for the emperor.

Fire and ice in one sword! raved the Chancellor, rattling
the *Eis* in the forged *Eisen*. And sun fused with moon, novel body
that burns though it coldly wanes, sang one illuminee locked away.

        So the emperor must instruct
        his flocking birds, tensing himself
        to winnow intelligence
        from hyperborean rains,
        his thighs whiten with the gift,
        light spits it, heat gilds it,
        instruction he must master
        before the storm slackens,
        Shun yielding his power
        to Great Yü:

        "Sun and moon
urge a burning blossom from fulfilled fire dawn on dawn"

>   And where this will take them
>   is an ancient path,
>   although through the furnace
>   of the heart's ashy
>   whitenesses, such holes
>   for foxes and for the birds
>   still whiter nests.

Joys of the Rich

A young owl-shouldered nobleman
    flexing his entitlements,
physicist, literary theorist, erstwhile
manager of the royal moneyers,
    with almond teeth and chapped lips.

What does he like to do?
    Disengage culture, lift it
above the cheeseflake contentions of the streets,
    nod at the square-torsoed ladies,
    wink at the fur-draped dancing girls, he
speechifying against "reality"
unless it too submit to the fictional,
    and then reclining
along the Bellerive under the Tinguely machine,
    leaping up when it burbles
        and running after all those pearls
the Emperor gave him, pearls and three white marksmanship medals
    dangling from a green sash.

Ministers and examiners
nod at him, winking, and the last one
taps him with an embroidered portfolio:
    "*Hoi* there, *Zauberlehrling*, welcome
        to the decades of dominion".
He wants to zoom out over Azure Lake
    but something is not working:
ministers and examiners stand there,
    staring at his brogans. But
this is only one stage, one phase, in the ordeal.
Come dawn, he will tower through mists
along the Limmat, his mansion the Old City, his doorway
    all of its oak panels, his chimney
        ten thousand chimneys
reeking above Protestant rooftiles. From them
    the slow smoke unfurls
        at his bidding.

Generosity swells his chest,
he throws silver at the feet of Old Jack
who plies the lower reaches of Bahnhofstrasse
    with flute and leather drum. And then
singing girls in battle array, leather
        seething under ring jangle
as they troop to their cubicles. He thirsts!
Tonight he will dine on a phoenix from Geneva
and have it out over the real-estate bubble.
        And he will cock the crossbow
from Zwing-li's chambers with one yank
    and shoot a bolt
        over the Kantorei's tower.

He knows the Guest Workers are here somewhere,
    under those river mallards
flaking their Greek of migration downshore –
    gamma, upsilon major...
        he imagines the weaver
    fancies them weaving, the carpenter
stretching a rafter over their long home.

When he hitches up his belt they roll forth,
Venetian epigrams and clean slates,
investment profiles from a cloudless sky
like green processors just learning to tweet.

Dissolving, and again dissolving,
    cloud over the capital of High Pastures
and flurries swirling
        off the peak of South Mountain,
the beauty sleep of darling Faust soothing him
as the suckling sorcerer rolls over and snores.

Ditty for Mayor Fu of Freiburg im Breisgau

Bronze yellowbill by the lake,
fat Mayor Fu,
you told us, venerable drake,
but who told you?

Clamorous on splayed feet
clacking, flapping,
announcing the black bomber fleet
a full day yapping –

old *b'iu b'iu*, your din
left you the lake's premier citizen,

of waters mirroring hour after hour
cloud drift and the winking
darkness and your nephews cruising unblinking
across the spire of the tower.

But our head-down diviners trudge now through glitter
turning over in the plage
bent on believing that art, even yours, is no transmitter
of messages,

and makes no claims, reaching
indeterminately, never quite beaching –

while this shimmer, your home, extends from shore to shore
about which connection
they float few inquiries, no detection
being called for.

When you dredge up gobbets from the depths,
occasional diver,
and spit them among piths
of the surface, both arcane as ox liver,

and we resume our query, old bird,
that question rummages
the attics and cellars of its own word
long since they rebuilt over the ravages.

And the present you will be drifting over,
pintailing its quiet,
will ripple its wide discourse of moved and mover
while we go on trying it:

"Who can be in stillness and, out of it
as well as through it, move a thing
onto the way, so that
it will come into its own shining?"

Rhyme Prose One

"What to do? While I speak, evil is busy, the living live pain".

First attempt: In the West, when peaks "were wed by fire in their embrace with the beyond, they flung a tough arm towards being – clotted by the high ice". Yet their mist-over-stone evanescence across the forms wove lattices over the first field, deep acre of wind and bone. Ice weeps in that tensional allotment of the *peregrini* where there is no place. There they converge and converse. Unrolling their plans, siting their city, then trekking off, they repeat the exchange: – Have you traced the route to the first capital, have you learned why they moved on and have you seen how they built it? – No, but lay out your memories. – It was set up in the one stable place, the surveyors stretched their star-web from range to range, the fountain overhead spread its streamers, the river below rinsed the rusted emerald of foundation.

Second attempt: The mountains behind the mountains, the peaks within the peaks – these were glimpsed by Dharmakara when he made his forty-eight vows, refusing the final consolation until a place in the West should come into being where sufferers might taste truth free of their suffering. Such is the one place. Yet before it rise the steeps of cold within coldness, summits vapored by deathless indifference, around voices pledged to protection while they publish their inventory of reality: "Well, that is the way hell is".

Third attempt:

Blow on blow tunes the chisel
while stone silvers the metal and the man.

A Hero's Life

Sun valves open blinds
in schoolrooms under an alp
and the stone academy
in a city, sun levers help
along each crack

while teacher imprints a pig
on penmanship, the error
obvious because
leads and erasers are out,
only wet ink is permitted,
it has got to be right before
it hits the page, slotted
in the grid millenially plowed
to a field's edge and turning
strictly. Small scaling to big,
dead with the still-aborning,
laws with outlaws, are true
as an edge is true...
                              the sharer
in all these is a squint-eye
assessing other kinds
of eyes for a coal burning
sullenly hidden, solar
glint on the Roman wrestler
in rooms that Gottfried Keller
gave his hero, its plaster
smoldering then catching,
igniting in him "the golden
ring of defense and attack"
after the others went off
was it laughter dribbling back?
the fatherly one having stuck
a fist through his large page
of inky abstract stuff
and that was his coming-of-age
the women giggling elsewhere
so the fellow begins sketching
all that musculature.
And none of this is soon over.

Rhyme Prose Two

For squaring posts from Grisons granite, *arbor sed non vitae*, to bear a gridwork of rafters suitable in all weathers and for the attachments of vines:

in the quarry face or the remnant block set in line at spacings of 30 cm holes to a depth of 12-15 cm, with star drill, the length of the desired slab.

This is called the adjustment of temperament to matter.

"Get Goebbels and Mueller!" Gisevius to von Stauffenberg. "I have thought of that". Von Stauffenberg handed a pass to Gisevius, brown scrip that squeezed him, transubstantiated him, to mentor Niemoller's side, the pastor and submariner still blinking in the light beyond Dachau, at Weissflujoch above Interlaken.

The Tyrolean guide brought the half-Jewish family up into stony *pastura alta*, then slipped away from them down the black slope, against his word.

Tamp hardwood pegs of the same diameter as the starrings into the holes, then soak in water.

Paired cognac bottles for *der Führer*, flying out of Smolensk. The mechanism cracked a vial of sulfuric acid, which ate through copper wire restraining the firing pin. Undressing the twin bombs later in his lap, Schlabrendorff found that everything, just as in Diderot's diagrams for the *Encyclopedia*, had gone off as it should. Yet there they sat.

Stepfather, sliding through moondark larches at the col, and Swiss private calling *Halt!* crouched mirrored, a half-closed claw.

When the slab has split from its parent face, repeat starring and pegging along the side.

"From Venezia. We have family, Geneva. Let me use a telephone".

Position in postholes, sash heads with chief members, test the trueing.

This is called the opening of world-space.

The wife fell as dead weight to the ground. On the soldier's shadowed face the daughter caught no sign. "*Ja, ja*. Over there. But two minutes, no more".

When the separation occurs cleanly, the report is carbine-like, as if underwater. Rims of the starrings fracture randomly, to either splay of the break-centering, ultraviolet and before breath has quieted.

For this condition there is no enduring cure.

Forged Heart Blade

His son dead, Meng Chiao had to put aside
the bow of mulberry and six tumbleweed arrows
shot by an archer in the four aimings at his birth.

And then refusing to eat the carcass abandoned by winter
he proscribed the knife of his own kindness – for on its point
his virtue would have stunk like dead meat.

Between the thing suffered and the sacrifice
stretch the snow ranges with their soundless
dead glare at storm lull over the last crossing.

Yet they are here, keen under crudded mantles
and sheathed in the beds of high lakes, here they
shall rest, swords heaved by priests and chieftains

into the ooze at dawn or sundown, and abide
in the protection of valleys they protected,
arduous to fashion, unblooded, of highest worth.

En Avant de nos jours

"In those days, clouds of unbridled sweetness
      will wrap the earth in sleek airs.
Theirs will be the breath of greening,
      of greening and seedtime".

As for what anticipated such developments,
already there are those among us
who can imagine it for themselves,
but they are not given to loquaciousness.
And so, good woman, spare us the details.
Those will be the days,
      yes indeed,
those will be the days.

Tally Stick

"A bit of sea" –
Joha waited a lifetime to hear
    this commencement
in a round of renga
so he could say "Mount Osaka!"

        Ford Madox Ford with fellow officers
        at *bouts rimés*
        in a dugout between bombardments:
        contested realities.

"A little birth" –
the other meaning, the overtone,
    Joha waited in vain
to catch from his partner, so he might
come back with: "words at the wedding".

        Pericles after the action
        upright in his utterance,
        upright, in its matching separation
        from the remembered action.

"Even in
an age gone
rotten
song's way goes
right on..."

        Even in the days of the magpie
        when the pen flies winking
        and the easy wind fattens many wings –
        even then the voice of the tortoise paves the long path.

    A bit of sea
a little birth
    Mount Osaka!
words at the wedding: indeed,
to hear these speaking each other, to the end.

Sotheby Parke Bernet Renga (muted)

On a lake balcony:
fourteen bronzes, fractured
apse mosaic (two saints),
and a stone Ganesh dancing,
lotus cupped in lower
left hand, staff in right,
serpent in upper pair
curving over the mounded
good luck of the ageless
elephant brow, and maidens
in each of the four corners,
one
      trilling a flute.

The Ascension in warped gold,
    contact wires
in each of the four corners,
back of glass spider-webbed
by tossed brick: the alarm
rang its Benedictus,
several celebrants
departed, several
     more converged.

,   In the several facades
of sparrow and investing gambler and
    Baudelaire's fly-blown hero,
hopping and peering and strolling,
a "congealed uneasiness".

   Hopping more than once
from the Met to a jet to this bank vault,
    Thomas Sawyer Hoving
was shaken, but not by remorse,
and "not for very long".

The hated Ezra Pound
asked us to try to read
the ways that colors in nature –
undersea purples veiling
a body that slowly deepens –
got worked into colors at hand
and fixed in non-portable
non-detachable stuffs,
a free man's length of wall
frescoed with arbors of justice;
that this is what the coppery
flame-eyed goddesses come to;
that this is where their earrings
light us, past the stalls
where nothing stands *hors de commerce*
for very long; that gloss
on color colors our innards,
that the gloss is the text is the treasure
and none of it is for sale,
and an eye, and an ear, they can hold it
with not a little effort,
and the four corners of things
get freshened by that outlay
and it's nothing to do with folklore,
and nothing to do with bankbooks
breeding, but everything
to do with the wine flare of gold
when eyes are the vessels, eyes
we have never quite looked into,
that do not offer themselves
and feel cold, hated and feared
eyes not ours to command.

A Sash for Wu Yün

O dropsical Augustus, your tuner the Great Woz
has outlived his time –
yet the Tao I studied begins, through cold hazes
of necessity, to spell its name.

Name! Soundless, not to be manipulated
by the clack-mongers.
So the administration was not impressed, being still delighted
to drape parrots on its singers.

My apologies, Li Po, I got you into that stew –
no way out but the ladle,
with old Cow Leasher, castrato, chief of staffless
ditherings and twaddle

lifting that spoon, pouring us out seriatim,
landing me in this hut.
But the Tao I aimed at begins, beyond even drums
of the rebellion, to show what's what,

and the cock I owe you shrieks its red silence,
and the rue I owe guards it,
and the honor our masters have tread out in obedience
wends towards it.

Who owns the thatch he must reclaim from sparrows
and bring his sky under?
Sidney and T'ao Ch'ien, the bow for your two arrows
bends in thunder gardens.

Prehistoric fellowship of wine, grain, feldspar,
anterior loves,
flares coiling into the void that floats our star,
are what, beneath quiet, moves.

Are what in the red cast of the stone head
and in its shut lids
and in the curves of its mouth, intimate the dead
coming to life in the gods.

Yes, hell is populous with administrators,
and deities get demoted,
and *communio sanctorum* swarms with agitators,
the ranks bloated,

and now they tell me that at White Cloud the Prior An
was incinerated
by his monks. From the Republic to Tien An Men
smoke drifts unabated.

They have plucked leaves from our Book of Great Peace
to fan those fires, but
the realized mind does not smolder, I take notice
in order to forget.

Yet, to serve as fig leaf over unwieldy parts,
can that be good
even for the leaf? A sage application disconcerts
because easily misunderstood.

Let them use us, but then let them build
on the brash diamond
at rough in the heart's flaw, and have its world
gyrate through the clan, and

have the whole spinning thing meet the infinity
of suns under and over,
all in the effort at hand, that quantity
set midmost, our mover.

Let, let... and let stoppages of thought
meet the solving rains,
let bookstores carry at least one world map, and let
the city clear the drains.

Sun bathes in the white east and that gorge seethes,
then couches in the long valley,
but its steam has purified how many worthies?
and which one keeps tally?

When the palace wing burned, virtue cried arson
but stood there without water.
A thrown chair folded itself into a picnic fire
where it fell, but not one person
showed any appetite, the daughter of Senator
Beautiful on Twelve Sides lay severed by a smoking rafter
and sold no tickets. Slowly it came to me
that all my affairs were present, and that the moment
was on fire. I sat down
before those embers, no one
paying me any mind.
Mei Bo got sliced and pickled, Ji Zi pretended
to be mad, but Wu Yün discovered
that alchemy was concrete and consequent
and every bit the roasting he had feared.
Each movement in the compound
I saw from a hawk's brain, and heard the full
orchestration of wind, men, and holocaust
note-perfect, while the hells
unravelled their aeons within minutes? Seconds?
When I looked up, the living sheen on her blood
had not yet gone glassy among the braids.

Fire sleeps in wood, only to be wakened
by the slumbers of men –
air wants to darken, in a bituminous
dream of the earth.

Let us pronounce benedictions over the wedding
of oxygen and chair stuffing,
over the transubstantiation of scholia and curtains
let us swing incense.

(May they not hurry the celebration, that filmy
entourage of breezes,
nor the eunuchs usher us, nor the best man be
Zeal of the Land Busy.)

Thereafter to this place, and my second hut,
the original a sacrifice
to lightning from the immortals, who will not let me squat
like some *perfectus*.

Standing in the ashes I saw monks sweating
up a hill road
with a wagon of bricks, joists, and tiles
for their monastery,
like the friars under Fra Leo
hauling stone up to San Francesco, to keep
the negotiable bones in place.
On my shelf near the classics, your letters,
and warblers past the threshold
I gauge by the acceleration of Aprils
timed by the plits from my eaves.
The summers becoming embers, I begin
to lose track of my poems on the histories.
The scrolls no longer beguile me,
not even John of Winterthur
totting up legends of the Emperor
who was to rise up from mincemeat
and scourge all baldpate instigating Franciscans
"who will smear cow dung over their tonsures
to hide themselves", while he harries
with a great host to Olivet
to yield up all empire at the dry tree –
now that would make a resounding ditty, but
it does not suit my mandolin.

Beyond the blood mists of force, I see ancient hands
go rung over rung
out of Climachus, the amor of Mozartean masons,
and smiths hammering.

See ancient faces float from the years' dark
in the eyes' brief dark,
shaping themselves as seeds not yet planted,
the quickening of work

cast back by dragons unwinding
as they tear me away –
cloud rope, hold me tight – and I watch my own steading
of earth burn beneath day,

the cyclone stilled, welded, in more than a dream of earth.
The palace has surrendered
to a web spun through one night by revolving fires,
and Merlin has wandered

among them, shedding their spell, speeding
past the defective ear
of Arthur, through gnats over a streambed in August,
shat through power

beyond the last throne, though he condenses to all those matters
he is meant yet to speak –
sun and moon, let me go – and at last mutters
into the glare, the break.

The Death of Yuri Andropov

In snow squalls over this hill, on a bridge, Lenin,
    in rooms above it Solzhenitsyn surrounded:
    "Your socialism may be as bad as you say
    but our socialism will be good!" Here Brecht recited
    then slyly exited, coordinates chalk the wind,
fifteen seconds to bundle them off the tram,
    handicapped herded by a few teachers –
    the prettiest woman, childless, wheeled a boy
    who laughed No! or cried out No! meaning it
    under Ignaz Heim in sandstone, Friend of Folksong.
Realism binds a spell around the matter
    obsessive matter incompleteness of the matter –
    balloons bobbed the drabbly Tennysonian
    locks for his centenary marked months late
    in the streaked mothy air No! they slanted
higgledy-piggledy up the High Promenade
    No! over a signed Cocteau unsold and oranges,
    Yoruba womb in ebony, smoked glass bank,
    and coffin in a tram keening down the cut, white cross
    floating on the sedate blood rectangle,
and hop-skipped as English Rock wailed
    from her radio No! while slowly into
    the barren woman a slim hull of colors
    berthed itself among quiet throngs, their pier
    bannered under scud low and sweeping.
Negation the first gesture, affirmation
    therewith a follower, this may be
    experimentally confirmed, yet it does not follow
    that choice has yet been born, only that
    its powers have at last seized on the clutter.
Crooner cut off, the boy's boots No! kept on
    flailing the beat, then snowy strings, "Pathétique"
    No! No! No! archepiscopal burble
    "Chairman Andropov passed on today in the Kremlin"
    lenses swelling his pooled eyes, flakes holding to them,
mittened girl whanging the wire fence among
    Yes! cloudy strings resuming, and under glass
    the brightness welled out, down his mottled cheeks as
    all drove white and one may begin to imagine
    her tears at last coming No! Yes! No! Yes! Yes!

Rhyme Prose Three: Chapter of the Nine Rocks

One aspect waves under the water face, it rephrases the tilts of her mazy phane, it is bearded with her shifting tints. Its contrary rears above such propositions, splashing, judging the flux and her agitations, denying with stance and essence that judgment begins on its own frizzled pate. The unitary aspect is no longer at hand, having been small and uncomely and shagged by an urchin into the offshore brightness, vanishing. But from there it imposes its terms, there it abides.

Drifting me into being, the heavens of water.
   Pouring from my brow, water's chevelure.
   Sluicing mind, the roaring intellect of water.
   Altering mind, the molecular zero cataclysm of water.
   Presiding over my undoing, the long hands of water.

Blasted to pieces, disjecta, together with my ancestors spread out abiding, yet from us the iron rim, the black tread, the bare heel of a child draw tone and rhythm. We sing.

I am tied neither to approaching totality, ecstatic concept, nor expanding view. My mineral horizon, such is totality. Here, now, the golden age.

In hot necessity my mother conceived me, in metamorphosis she brought me forth. Hard in thy hand I am, in Him am nothing.

To be poured out is not my prayer, for I have been, but to occupy space as the correspondence that can inhere only there, and all that it can be there. *There* even your great Kant swerved on himself, mind not on but in the unity of object, for there is a coercion involved. There is here.

The larch splitting my side sentinels the stream cooling my fury.

My white mantle shrouds a removal from history which lets me assess it. And this is what you marvel at: not the icy carapace, but the crystalline discipleship.

The one finding his way to me will uncover in my cave the skull of his first similar, and the trickle of saving blood rusting its sutures, and the onset of storm, through eclipse and downbreaking flashings, in the twelfth hour ever approaching. But he will find too that the crown of my hill presages alterations with the breath of browsing deer I seem to remember from before time, auguring a last great change. He will find the exiled path of the stone.

"Vega over the rim of the Val Verzasca"

Vega over the rim of the Val Verzasca
and a mountain heaped from night with house light in it
    make a vast cave over man.

I have mislaid Rome, and the long house of Greece
has slipped my grasp, I am motionless.
In the eye's cavern, in the ear's dripping chamber...
    hunters brushed at wet space
    arching them overhead:
    endless, those recessions.

And on a mountain, when the last evening
    trades fuzzy dusk for totality
and stone ledges are everywhere our door,
    and we are set free in the house
to run, loll, knock over the ochre pots
    where bloods of gift achingly flower –

    yet as it was with the commanding
        Florentine, so even now:
        the color of all this
        has passed when I feel it come home,
        and even it, while it speaks,
        has not yet witnessed the end.

Clam Shell with Hunting Scene

Resolving autumn, and by Rhine flood
vine-hung bunkers kneel among shore ripples.

      Lather and branch lash, white tail tuft

Where the hunter, still and then leaping, is renewed bloodrush
paced by the ever-valving and shuttering deep iris.

      Quarried companionship, pursued gift

Justice with headsman's axe slides among shades of
justice with sashed gaze and all-bearing shoulders.

      String longing for the shaft

Ravenous paws of the maples scooping, cuffing at
the chance wing, arrows from the water, quarry from the heart.

      No rehearsals, the act has begun, is swift

Spot weld by the missile caught side-on running, there is
no leakage of the message fused by flesh into mind,

      A value fugitive and feeding, the dripping pike gaffed

spending itself in the breech nova, the shell empties
so that emptiness may take hold in matter's long wall.

      Cliff its seam, vein its rift

Variations in the constancy of union
recalibrated where ten arcs crossed and the bronze rested,

      The gone heft gaining weightlessness

but thrust beyond motion at one flicker by the meaning
no beast anticipates and no man does not.

      weightlessness at the top of its loft

Bronze edge, lead ball, steel borer and splayer, heart's harrier,
shall you weave coats from the storm to cover a stranger made welcome?

    Hammer, stone, eye and eye, warp, weft

But the last miniscules I cannot make out, the great hand hurried them,
O Father I am small, and through long watching may grow, but not
                                                                                            larger.

"Fifteen stars fence polar fire..."

Fifteen stars fence polar fire, the moated wall mirrored them,
songs from that palace have not yet found the tomb,
but now our body is a ferment, many where one was,
its form stretches beyond sight and will know no ease,

the sinuous line of the violin pushing alone
into the next spaces, darknesses up and down,
married not implausibly to the mourning, hammering
clubfoot of the great drum.

Shouting matches between Buddhist and Jesuit,
mind's fountaining fire against mind mirroring it,
shatter. Where that glass was, night's acreage
spreads to meet returning light and labor's dull rage.

Into spring fields, to turn up flint bits of first man!
But one must wait for rain to baptize the worked stone,
yes, wait for the plough, then for downpour, then go
head hung forward through fragrant furrows.

What were their hopes? To build a house for the ages.
The four provinces of time a stone seat for judges.
Their ship of feasts was keeled longer than a fortress,
splinters from its ribs shine up through this loess.

Where lines between watchfires crossed they laid out our themes,
as a bird through night's dome again and again aims
through origin to destination. What has pushed
their themes upon ours? Flint flakes, the soul is not finished.

Bird Garden

Albertus Magnus clambered inside the armillary sphere
    to slip-tuck the ecliptic ring – the sun had been tracking erratically –
    and found the stratosphere so much to his liking
    that he craned in the whole dome of his scriptorium.
Had he known that architects unleashed by the Revolution
    would puncture somnolent caves of masonry
    with spannings of the planets and the principal shiners,
    he would have stayed away. As it was
    he soon grew restive and aggressively
    redesigned his robe, stitching in oak leaves, grape tendrils,
    and the forepaw signatures of the greater mammals.
Had he known that Jacques-Louis David, and then Vladimir Tatlin,
    would be enlisted to constume their confrères
    in the uniforms of liberty and belonging,
    he might have pricked his thumb. As it was
    he guessed, with the primitive ardors of the sage,
    that a surplus was called for.
With straightedge and angle he churned out section and plan for windmills.
    He confected savory names for their stems, cogs, bevels, vanes, and creakings.
    He connected contrapuntal cloud drifts and he distilled elixirs.
    Finally he rebounded to his forte, classification and intercalation.
    Labored, he did, over the whole orchard weave of it. But ah,
    his new mechanism, the cosmic arbor, still lacked animation.
Then it happened, three lady partridges flew past.
    Grabbing brush he lodged them, swift and level, on the arch of his trellis.
    With them the wind entered and remained,
    the scene crossed over and inhered,
    the ensemble breathed.

"When Morning Star penetrated the lower spheres
    he found the Keeper of the Air and commanded:
    Open the gates of air! and they blew open.
And boring down farther he found the Keeper of the Waters and commanded:
    Swing wide the flood gates! and they whelmed open.

Sweeping through, going deeper, he found the face of the earth sub-
                                                          merged by seas.
   And striding below them
   he came upon two fishes lying there on the face of the waters,
   and they were yoked together, holding the wide world
   at the command of the Unseen One.
Going lower again he found broad cloud cradling ocean vastness,
   and still he descended, and found his own hell,
   the furnace of Gehenna, after which he could penetrate
   no farther, at impasse before the force of those flames".

No partridge, this underfellow of our aeon, winged unhitcher of the
                                                               Fishes.
   But every garden has one.

Vox altivoli volatilis
   intoned Scotus Eriugena before men, climbing after the eagle of John,
   but curved within the wax of his cell he buzzed over the emptiness
   of *umbra*, trailing that dark path past our light
   until across it flew the unnamed, and he broke out:
"Every creature will be turned back into shadow, that is to say
   towards God, as a star near the rising sun".
   Obscurity fuller than our shining.
"Things that exist stem from those that do not exist"
   and from Mind that is not. Dear Alumnus, the nihil of the prime
   works not through subtraction, but pouring from the source,
   engendering, shadowed with eternity.

"While John sat stroking a partridge, a hunter stopped, amazed.
   – Aren't you John? You, fooling with a bird?
   John looked at him. – What is that in your hand? – My bow.
   – Why don't you carry it strung? – It would grow slack
             and be useless when I needed it.
   – Exactly. It's the same with me, son, so don't fret over my pastime.
   If my mind couldn't play this way, it would never spring in the hands
             of the spirit".

"While John sat there, a partridge flew down and played in the dust at
                                                                                                                   his feet.
                     John watched and watched.
A priest who had heard him saw this and said to himself, *Hmmph!*
John saw his thoughts. – Maybe you should study this bird at play,
                                                                                                                           my boy.
Who do you think brought you here anyway? because I don't need
                                                                                                                  some partridge
flopping around in the dust. That partridge
       is your own soul".

Could it be that John was playing with a partridge, no one else there,
   printing his nonpointing fingers with feather-jostled dust, saying not
                                                                                                                       a word?
"Those gone lines and tipped markers: where are the acres now?
Wherever the partridge calls, the greening begins, blooms come".

Novissima Sinica

Smoke drift from the Somme and Verdun
disclosing the black cumulus of Monsieur le Science
towards which the sons of Newcomen and Curie
    stagger without conviction.
Sheltering from a downpour in a Cambridge bookshop
and drunk on Godwin, Shelley, Hamilton, Cavour,
    Xu Zhimo comes home to Pater.

Trail after Russell to London! Russell lingers in China.
Sniff at the new blooms of Lowes Dickinson!
Petals crumbling to guitar dust in pine shadow,
    massacres by new warlords
assuaged by draperies in *The Virgin of the Rocks*,
famine inhumed with bluets in the middle distance.
    Xu hankers after banking.

Turn, pastor errante, now that you are educated,
prosecuting your divorce, a Zheijang Milton,
get on the boat and go back, lecture in English
    on the quadratics of change.
Shall we count the heads mounded in village squares?
Shall we gauge turnover at the top of the new scramble?
Xu pedals fast over the Cambridge fens into sunset
    in order to prolong it.

Round Trip Chanties

The scholar soared to American
scenes on a flying tiger.
Next to him, an informant.
"Do? I own an airline,
fifteen planes. We transport
cadavers, we scatter ashes,
but our biggest take comes from
murderers. Yes, we move 'em –
equipment is always full,
triremes, closed-circuit TV,
agents seeing them off,
cops waiting on the runway".
Below, a young blond couple
paraded up a creekbed,
hair and sackcloth streaming.
There was so much to learn
and so little time in which to
etcetera. "Here, my card".

Next to him one cycle before
the crash of 'eighty seven,
an economist harnessed
to the incumbent Filial
Incorruptibles, and sweating hard.
Under the Han, a general dreamed that his sleeves
grew down to the ground; his chair shaman
put a royal face on this ill fit.
Then the general dreamed that new windows
had been installed in the palace, though upside-down.
These his counselor managed to conjure into
proper perspective. But when the general
usurped the throne and swiftly led his people
into tribulation, the sage let on
that there was still one more way
of looking at those omens.
What coat-trailer enjoys trimming
the tails he has had to ride,
the hems of the man with the knife?

Sorting Straws

A crystal into the salt swirl... and it begins
where there had been nothing
between light and the eye, ladders springing
over whirlpools to hang

anchored among handclasps, those glistening
scaffoldings that turn
into structure, acrobats cartwheeling entire from
the homunculi of pattern.

But realignments have invaded death, catalyzed
by crime past the scale
of speech that held it, beakers shattered and the wave
carrying off the wall.

So that speech itself has asked itself to fall quiet.
And with it duty,
knowingness flapping like a loose tarp, each pirate
taking booty –

but do these have us wait for the doe, her grassy jaw
pausing as the eyes lift,
who waited for no corps de ballet, her step
the unseizable gift?

Duty quiet still knows ashes sifted with generational
sands of the river
and the pine branch it reset for a hammock to attune
some last cover,

duty looking beyond quiet looks to unlatch
a gate opening on
that high bridge conjured over the tumult by each
tenaciously held tone.

Lan or thoroughwort is no orchid, but "orchid"
is what we get:
rough word! Pull up hawthorn roots and you grasp thornbush,
leukakantha thrust wet

into contests of candor, whiteness outdoing white
in the brutal swings
of renovation, or in the prickly savagery of ideas sniffing out
the staleness even of things.

Yet shades of that noncolor: what shadows them
burns farther than away,
as the spring's root and the wind's mouth stem open from
le dieu caché.

If they orchestrate "monkey's tube trouser tatters
codpiece drying stain"
while lenses veer towards the dead moons of Neptune, craters
dilating the screen,

there still oozes from all this some physical
or metaphysical sepsis
which they only half-credit, a putrefaction nine times
their own encapsis

of the required art, for more than their knives now
addresses the corpse
plump or bony, smooth or hairy, scalpeling whatever
in the soul usurps.

The soul too can be false, charmer incapable
of sweating long enough
to distill sure potions, or of putting them
surely to the proof.

Novel histories of the passions flutter decayed pages
and so, that day no further,
that year no deeper and that lifetime no freer of the rage
dragging the groove or taut tether.

In wheelchair limbs banked coals break to embers,
but shall we then know
the anatomy of loves bent past our reach? O Herd Boy,
there are galaxies to go.

On his knees before a deer, a hermit has proposed
creature to creature
neither devotion nor daftness, but attention, and she attends
though he will never teach her.

Were they to follow my hand through its brush tip's
elixir spreading
into hair, raven's cry, parting at morning, would they
still dispute while reading?

The within of the immeasurable firms, and I have
touched you at last,
and this warmth signals from lastingness, even as you give
form to what has been missed.

"And what do they do..."

And what do they do when they are lost in themselves?
Sit on benches, stand in grass and watch sails.
Stare forward, elbows on knees, at hells revolving.
Is this in a garden, or out in the blown waste?
From a hill the resting soldier saw plumes of earth.
The hermit asked, "What are they doing down there?"

Day has advanced. And to one turning back
in inquest of the day, as did Holbein
Skull son of Skull, to claim his father's brushes
and scaffolding and the gold paid in fee,
they will say, "The cloister has burned down.
Go, if you wish, dig gold from the ashes".

Day leans forward. The babe of time in his brain
pings with a small hammer against the wall
tick-tick. Soon peasants will come heaving torches.
Yet how the father's hand rewets and smoothes
powders of berry and bark on the groined curves.
And cowled singers file in to take their stations.

Hazelnut

Instead of perfectly evading us
the power swole and burst like a hazelnut
set in the fire, all the while holding shape
in his mind, as he wrote to his father Leopold.
So it can be. And so then came the unfolding
through sketches during the hot carriage rides
towards after-dinner card tables, the Prinzessin's,
to improvise among the unhearing. But once
the Landgrave set down his ivory toothpick,
staring at nothing, taken by the modulations,
the fragrant stink from his ceramic pipe
in trilling swirls, the musketry at Salzburg
and Amalia's hair long ago. Those also
smolder, also delay within the broadcast
efflorescence not wholly held in score
or serially decaying minds of those seated
in curved rows to listen, there or here
or in future, no more than in one stab
of the sky zigging down between cool firs
rimming the slopes he scanned from the swung carriage,
he has been telling me one thing all this while,
or in reedy whine of shrapnel off stone
at the bend of that road when another brain flared out
to sink like his unregistered in the field,
hearing – it enters between the shoulder blades – the river
of cloudy light, wet granite, and starmoss dirt.

Fantasia for Du Bellay

Fevered a second time, going farther under,
I saw the rooflines of Rome drifting above me
on the early walk to work, no
others in the streets, a holiday.
Foreigners with foreign boss miss the privilege.

And then saw priests and prostitutes and felines,
those permanent residents, trailing home through
still empty prospects, tirelessly
themselves, and timeless in the light that wrapped them,
Du Bellay's century with Pasolini's.

But cursed and honored first by the young Frenchman,
one hundred lines for a cat! So there it was, then,
from one in the cousin cardinal's
employ, that hairy tailpiece for proportion.
Yet the fire hadn't finished with me, I waited,

carried at first, then winding through Italy,
threading frozen passes, thus now the Frenchman,
and lodged at a mill, the darkness
torrential, timed by the thudding of a great wheel,
France not far, but chills eating through gunny sacks:

to that poured rhythm, shapes of France's future
swam before him, and of the church's also,
though in that hour staying
only to sear the satirist and forsake him;
and then a woman's voice, foretelling his deafness.

Osip Mandelshtam in the Grisons

Wings sickling meadow frost – were
harvests along the way to his "hills of mankind"
this urgent? So little time to prepare
    that long meal for the mind

    which, though they stole it, he could rebuild –
plow-spill, honey, or blood's gold under the skin,
the soul's abysses craving their arches, filled
    by cross-ribs groining in.

    Sceptics claim that he never went,
anymore than he ever mastered German.
Italy! Clearing through hazes, ocherous tent
    for the spirit's Europe of Russian.

    There are the eyes of time
        the time never has,
    and there are colors brought home
        from wandering in the gaze,

    but it wouldn't be long before high ice
was Russian murder, and binoculars
in one's helpless hands, powers of the Zeiss,
    reached out for other powers.

    In looking towards the high sluices
of a dry stream, reconnoitering advance
alone up its bends, there was the sibilance
    of waters to win, real voices.

    Laughter cascading from below,
pressure for days in the chest easing in speech,
the builder's mute heave and balancing, all go
    through us and out of reach.

    Through, but that passing makes the span,
the architecture, the materials,
and the thing bearing their crushing weight is man,
    a slight thing in their scales.

>There were the eyes of time
>>the time put out,
>and there were colors of time
>>the time did without,

>and it wouldn't be long before mountains
>of a steel man pyramided the skies –
>but like Goethe refusing any lens,
>>Joseph used human eyes.

>The art of peoples? If that's your horse troop
>of insomniacs churning the earth to war
>or poetry, there's still the swallow's loop
>>and the quarry it twitters for.

Wind Under Sash, Val Ferret

Night-stuttering glass, a brisk hexameter
    as if the shade of Rudolf Borchardt passed
self-refugeed again, not singular in that honor
    yet alone out there,

carrying on his back the evening purples of the Mantuan
    and the ladder cliffs of Alighieri
back into Italy, back into the dishevelled, shaken
    atelier of the villa,

not as gods in his rucksack, nor the images of gods,
    not as *lares* but as the icons of men
carrying them, themselves carriers – for the clouds
    raked by the peaks

admitted only the most portable pieties
    and promised cyclone over anti-cyclone
of our new rain, saint clown seer duke *bona fides*
    of the types of the peoples,

amazon skull-smasher demoniacal berserker
    social democratic emperor
sculptor manipulator-of-masses-in-bulk worker
    plunging to the far plain,

paladin pastor pathfinder toppled out of the human
    to the primaries of a pre-world –
but trekking down, there was a German and a man,
    his paces still spacing them.

As if the shade of Borchardt rattled the sash:

even before the fist of the subjugator could squeeze him
    onto the roads, he numbered all the hands
to be hacked off, and went, not giving in to his doubt
    that the rope he would rappel onto

might have been jerry-rigged over that jumble down there...
    and in that moment let me suspend him
as the fist of the folk did, not alone though singular,
    rhizome dangling in the unrooted.

Rhyme Prose Four

The infant is buoyed by black smoke. And whose bairn is this?
   Lashed in green swaddling across a plain board,
      attended by sweatbright cradlers of bronze blade, by puffers on tusks
            of the ram or mammoth trumpeting through pine web.
   For nurses he has hyenas licking themselves, prowling, cosseting
                                                                      fleas,
   he bawls for no breasthold nor do his eyes blur. And he looks out at us.

And who are his protectors?
   Kindlers of fires here in the glade and there in a village,
   their skins ruddy, ashen, oily, varieties of one species,
   three who sought no star and waged no journey, no gift-bringers
                                                                            these,
   though they celebrate, crouch-prance, cousin him around among
            slouch and whinny of sly pelt, the far wood no refuge.
   They are nature moving towards blind completion,
   he is completion's pip thrusting back into nature,
   and the dominion twisting one of their mouths senses the curb of that
            law, grazes it, hovers. Towards us the small one stares.

And his hopes, his chances?
   Their kin he is, yet is not: unnumbered in the childermass, wilder.
   Crystalline forms of these his companions glitter in furnaces, shine in
                              caves of punishment and lack. Therefore
   he floats mast-lashed to a papoose rack, the smoked abiding seed.
   The chemical pleasures farmed in this our garden corrode
   visibility but not vision: wayfarer of the miniscule, already you have
                                                    budded from Krakatoa
   and I am learning to ferry you through the lid's wink,
   to beach you on the slopes of your assaulted growth
   where a troop of demons rings you in the equilibrium
   demanded for your balance, your intact pirouette.
   They will kneel to you, blowing bubbles windowed with towers,
                                                                    treasuries,
   piping you, from their illimitable embouchure, cap and bell and hunting
                                                                          horn
   and roistering lordship, surpluses of safety all
   evaporating. Pook! while the scene that already had appeared stays:
   oxide of expectation tints none of its recessional blues, it is not

sulfate of fulfillment exploding among those walls, nor do the cindery
pillars
climbing out of them, layering dusk, sift chaste flaws through future
ambers.
But from hiddenness something has come, has anyway arrived, is
what
looks out at us, and so from a phosphorous I glimpse edge-on and not
always
a child peers out along the slow fuse of continuance.
I, Ernst Georg Rüegg, have seen this in the thirty-fifth year of my age
et in pars fecit anno domini nineteen hundred eighteen.

Fleurs d'essence

Centaur, master of heroes,
    I recognize
your black bike helmet, but when
did you strap it on your back,
    that violin?

    With Helen
riding him again, disreputable
    Chiron

    guns it past Hakuin,
half warrior, half mystic, who oils each
    link in the chain.

German-speaking Peter, with fiddle conjured
on his back by Our Lord and sent into the tavern
    where they clamored for a tune,
denied he was any fiddler, at least three times,
    so they beat him and threw him out.

The Ancient spread her illegibles on a café table,
riding boots, student days, and Hitler among cut flowers,
then paused outside before two motorcycles
patting them: "I should like to give each of them a name,
but I should have to get to know them better first".

Seventh Moon

They say that once each cycle
    all of the gates open,
the under-gates, country wide – who could swing them? –
and high crystal fixities, pivoting:

and even the wall wanderers,
    those unburied ones, interrogated
but released into non-meaning,
    even they swim through and speed on –

and all the replays, didactic
    insistencies in slow motion,
lips intoning, and eyes
    rewinding the unrepealable,
cease when deer bend at the pool's edge
    and look across to the man reading
not from a book but his own fiber,
    from its grain wherever it has swung
on the small hinges of action –
beginning to read, that is,
    long after the pratfall
he managed in blood and inefficacy
by listening for the grindings of hell in the distance
then trying to haul back his mother's damned soul –
long after he got up
    by pressing against the dust
and then readjusting his robes
    before making a cloud exit:
all that comes before his looking into the living text.

•

When the Wall came down in Berlin
    the orchestras performed Beethoven,
letting the wind bands in the villages
    be heard, and dances, in the villages.
There is the unity from below, unstoppable.
But of the misted union
    between dead and living,
unsearchable, we may
    still ask: does it sharpen

at the behest of the living or the dead?
And we must ask: what of
              prolonged suffering
cancelled at a stroke by the gates opening?
Among the dead, they say,
      it lifts in purgation.
But among the living?

              •

The man who read under the deer's gaze had taken the tonsure,
formerly the boy known as Turnip, and he was a good boy
but he also wanted to go on a journey, so he went,
yet his mother only pretended to feed the poor, and so
came to wander the hells wailing for sustenance
gliding like reflections in stuffed shopwindows, famished ghosts.
Turnip was a good boy, but he rolled around on the ground.
"Get up! Set out bowls heaped with rice, pine nuts, roast fish".
Thereafter the king stipulated that his ministers
bring from the treasury platters of agate
brimming with red petals, and amber with greenwood.

Therefore at moonrise
      the older hills climb out of clarity,
therefore the fields are taken in
      from the spent ground and folded,
at dawn the mists lift from them
      over a battalion of shadows
          sliding brighter.

              •

The ford of souls ever
      was a tricky passage,
even here the king's nephew chooses white water
      when he stabs his king.
                      Even under
improved conditions there is something
      disconcerting about this transit.
When the revolutionary fallen were to be reinterred
      at the column, Place de la Bastille,

"Entrez, sublimes victimes!
gloire et triomphe..."
Berlioz framed the hearse bearing fifty coffins
with a wind band of two hundred
and wings of massed voices and strings, "Something
they can HEAR",

but twenty-four horses pulled raggedly
and the hearse swayed and tipped,
the procession stalled and they all cheered
Louis Phillipe on his balcony,
the clarinets paled unless trees
happened to reflect them,
and the strings lagged,
and at the climax
the Legion of the Guard stood dropping in the heat
and the sergeant major in his mercy had them step off
to fifty unmuffled drums,
blotting out
the choral apotheosis.

•

Richard Strauss on the podium
under a dome's oculus,
night pantheon of the swooning ear
and organ pipes in phalanxes
behind the percussion –

therefore the Reich's filmmaker, panhandler
of the cavernous, the swimming,
panned to a blond gaze and low bodice
as her eyes valved shut
over her own image of those pipes;
overlayed it with her beddable face *in exstasis*,
each bourdon, each stem of vox humana
towering in perspective,
lacking only the fins to home them in on their hits.

    And her eyelids darkened with blood shadow,
               young matron of death,
        while the old sorcerer led them
under the night eye of the dome into one rhythm,
        pantechnicon smoother of the long beat
               in the ongoing
          convergence of the arts,
    snowy-haired Strauss on the podium.

•

Carnevale trombones blatting down their arcade:
at the focus of the Piazza San Marco
        maskers heaped trash and torched it,
exceeding the scale permitted by regulations
and so drawing gendarmes to the perimeter,
      yet there are also regulations
traditional with the Most Serene Republic
setting the time elapsed before its gendarmes
          may move against bonfires,
said fires having their privilege at this season,
      but the enforcers stormed the piazza
before their stopwatches stipulated it, and so
          halfway out they hesitated.

At which time the maskers, attired also
    as gendarmes, bolted from their pyre
but froze in mimicry,
        the two fraternities
standing at impasse
      while the blaze towered.
    Rippled column of air,
arcade and roofline swimming as the heaped visibles
    twisted towards the invisible
from the crackling of an era swiftly rumpled –
    from the focus of stalled choruses
        crouching mirrored
around climbing flame through flame climbing.

•

And the fires in this sacrosanct foolery
      thrust aside altar candles
or yardarms and radar nibs
      sparking the storm's tooth, corposant,
or the burning inside Daigu, Great Fool
      when the mother whose boy he had buried
asked, "Where has he gone?" and he stood speechless
      then left for the tracklessness of the high places,
or even the fire set by a warlord around monks,
one of them blurting, "Where is the eternal?"
      with his master answering, "Right here,"
and the other pressing him, "But what IS it here?"
      and as the flames rose, "If you have done your job,
coolness will climb to you even out of this fire".

●

When jubilation crackles from those whose fathers
buried their crimes under a parking lot, this
      is a tone in the teeth of the wind.

Early today in the villages
      bandsmen stamped in the squares,
breath white as they moved out
under a baton towards the base line of hills
      where Sirius, or Sothis, or the dog
notches over, timing the gait,

the first star that we found with its dead twin,
      presiding jointly over flood and sirocco,
Sirius and its dark partner in dance
not themselves listening, yet gauging
      whatever in us may be listening
          for the living.

Spring Housecleaning

Flares from Beirut, North India,
and the West Bank
through one more May
of pink candles and white
down the chestnut avenues.

Pebble blossoms, paved
before the shut calyx
of the madhouse door,
red geranium
petals blown over them.

Kneeling at matins on one
good leg, one peg leg, a man
tamps cobbles into sand,
and it is not the stones ringing,
it is his hammer ringing.

Rhyme Prose Five

Get them off the bus at a country inn and seat them at long tables in the shaded courtyard. Put the groom, who has a talent for this sort of thing, in front of the others at his own table, pink booties snugged puppet-like over his hands, a knitted pink cap on his crown. Seat the bride behind him, blindfolded, and move her arm – bare, and showing evidence of hard work – around him to the platter of applesauce and crumbly cake. Stand the others, already laughing, in a semicircle offering no chink for escape, and equip them with cameras. The booties flail in unison. Most of the provender goes in. What fails to falls in his lap.

From the zone below fog-line, ravens sail in swing arcs towards the crannies where nests fit, but female eyes with vertical slits opening on deep fires send the raiders back out into their glide.

In a workshop below timberline crammed with windfall, work the chisel around the curl of a pine older than the nation, to the unfurled heads of the eagle and her young warrior. In her claw, set eight per cent or more of the weapons production for *das dritte Reich*. To be released on demand.

Colgan over Cogitosus, or Kan Pao Prosimetrics

Let the following not be composted:

That royal Dubthach lay with his slave Broisech, and as they rattled by one morning the axle sang out under the king's weight, and a druid said, "See who that is!" and his people told him it was Dubthach, but he said, "No, I mean the woman behind him", and he asked her if she was in the family way, and she gave him a straight answer, the future mother of Brigit, and so he said to her: "It will be a girl, and she will shine in earth as the sun does overhead".

That in his lust for the word young Prince Columcille stole a parchment Testament and started a blood feud that killed hundreds, and so began his long penance of exile, which ended with the old white horse weeping on his mortal breast, as the Grey of Macha nuzzled Cuchulain bound bleeding to his stone pillar.

That Kobayashi Issa, tending his father's old age, saw two young stags licking night frost from their fur.

That furious Francis cursed Brother Swine as Christ did the hapless fig tree, so that his innocent bristles and acquisitive eyes would crackle in the ultimate fires.

That the followers of Francis, cooped up in a sweat lodge and left there, saw a fireball in a chariot sailing around the room, and came to suppose that it was himself visiting them, little Ezekiels greasing the axles of the Merkavah, venerators of the second Elijah and the second Jesus, and not, therefore, themselves about to come down very soon.

That when young Lu was grilled by experts like the beardless Christ before the rabbis, he pleaded only patchy mastery of the scriptures, begging to be let off with the five elements and the ancestors. And they gasped, for these are the greatest test.

That the woodcarver delegated to replace the chipped head of Pharaoh chasing his Jewish hodcarriers across the great doors at Santa Sabina affixed the profile of Buonaparte.

That in one Sutra the prodigal, still wandering, came to a place where his father had gotten rich, and the father, secretly recognizing him, sent messengers, but the son got scared by this treatment, and so the father took him on as a hired hand and let him work his way to the top, and adopted him, only then holding the celebration and showing his hand.

That Mrs Thrale consented to whip Dr Johnson in the privacy of his chambers and before the eyes of God.

That Alighieri, handed a choice book in a druggist's at Siena, sat down to read and never remarked the loud *festa* trooping by outside.

That Matsuo Bashō, while walking and walking, and spotting a horse-chestnut tree on the outskirts, remembered Saigyō, the monk who wore thin his sandals on the footpaths of the islands, and who had composed lines about gathering chestnuts in mountain forests. And that Matsuo dropped then and there into etymology, inscribing the Chinese for chestnut, *kuri*, in the language of a land beyond that compounds "tree" and "the West", this last the land past all termini, where no blossoms fall. And that he then named Amida's Land but left Saigyō unnamed – Sai-gyō, west-going one – for, if the unapproachable is to have its cognomen come into shelter under the named tree, then and there pointing to the not-there, then the shadow brother, the foregoer and word handler, the hidden companion, would stay undisclosed. For that one has left the tree, with his naming it, here and behind, to go there. The names requisitely stay here, rooted and mortally blossoming. Whereas the companion has preceded.

That Niklaus von Flüe, abandoning wife and children near Sachseln to gaze into the night sky of the mountains with hot black eyes, saw a hideously wrathful face, and was shaken, his own face twisted. Later a beggar came in gold-flecked bearskin with a veiled brown face and eyes black as the lodestone and a voice pouring like an organ, "I come from out there, where the summer sun rises", and a mountain flattened itself to reveal the hosts of the other world, a mountain belonging to Odin. This time the face was drenched in love, honey-full, although the bear heroes and berserkers carry the holy fury of Wotan and the bear's wrath, and there remains the fact that in these mountains the great wanderer had always been old Wotan, and that he sang richly, Wotan the revealer and striker-open of the stony places. So this was Christ: here Bruder Klaus finally had his interview.

That a beam of light through a bowl of water brings to the ass of Balaam a new voice, while to the historian of Böhme it conceives only one more *"bâtard du christianisme"*.

That the rose peony, disclosing the infoldings of time and that essence which evades human affairs, lies out in the layerings of the law.

Anti-dithyrambics

He only wanted to sleep, that wakeful
professor among the ridgey pastures,
    he only wanted to lie down
  and snore like the hired hand sprawled
wholly this side of a searing command.

Through the car's headlights, a grey crone
    pushing a milk can on wheels:
  what Zarathustra caught in his high beams
was at first merely an old man of the woods
but at last the greybeard voltage that sizzled him.

  Under the sweep of headlights
    the flank of a red thresher
still chewing across the dark field:
behind, virtues churning sightlessly,
ahead, the massed clans of black grasses.

The inconceivable marriage was here consummated:
  the lonely one with his thunder eggs
    and a milky wraith off the peaks.
But their children are not our lame wolves in lamb's fur,
their terrible bairns do not clamber back into old forms.

Reading Western Masters

When Sokrates drew up his drugged leg
   a Vedic swan achieved lift-off,
     separating worlds
while its trailing web stuttered farewell to water.

Riverbed maidens, pressing your noses against
   the upper membrane, what codices
     could be yours, what mythologies, yet
there you must stay: realms there are, and guardians.

Hunters' dreams are sedulous to mark them –
as when a mallard, skimming in to land,
shoulders deployed like a nikë's, caught an arrow
through its foot, and the archer bagging it
told himself he could not have really killed it
that way, it must have been dead already. Yet

only one agency, blooded, leathery,
links water and the sky, supple whether
tucked away or spread for the gliding impact.
Therein tenses a connector, therein
also dangles a great wound, and through it
with swift archaic aim pierces our chance.

A Gross of Poems Linked in the Mixed Manner

1   Cubical interferences in clouds of summer,
        steel rod angled off the pole
    clasping the flap of red announcement.

2   Foam over the rim
    after a fast pour,
    soulful advice that smacks
    of promissory notes.

3   *Ein Blick ins Chaos*
    and that would be the sound of it, too – looking towards
        the flash over roofs, years,
    past candle and Nicholas soaring
    over sailors in their swamped boat.

4   Brecht, who never stayed anywhere
        very long, stayed
    in Herrliberg, with radio and ashtray
    and a Chinese painting on the wall
        that could be rolled up.

5   July haying under way
    on slopes of a valley
    opened only in this century,
    men pitchforking heaps
    and riding them downhill

6   while a red medical helicopter
    thrumbles far below
    carrying off a man
    who failed to jump
    fast enough from his tractor.

7   No plaque, "Goethe slept here",
    for the street musician
    with orthopedic frames
    and garden swing rusting
    on his filthy back.

8 Between inscribing
Pontius Pilate our abyss
  and Christ the human future,
Lavater looked up to see his young fan Goethe
skinny-dipping in the Limmat, chased by police.

9 With top hat, velvet frock coat,
  and gilded stick
a personage forges through morning fog on the Minster Bridge
but even he comes after Luther, and so cannot
  secure a General Dispensation.

10 If there be Unnatural Thinking,
it follows: there must also be Natural Thinking.
Infamy of the court painter, Piero di Cosimo:
he let the grass grow in his front yard.

11 In every chartered street I smell
Arabia Deserta's oil,
high tree withers, avalanche gathers, and down toil
ten thousand villagers
into every chartered street.

12 The one-man band,
seeing the cop draw his sword,
  exercized
that capacity known as
the Science of Absence.

13 Wagnerian businessman, puffy
  black velvet beret,
gets a measuring sidelong glance
from the Kabbalistic gardener in
  compact blue tam.

14 Thus Celan rebukes Brecht
  for chromaticism,
obvious banging of the intervals,
reproves him with spare leafage held up
  on the pruned limb.

15   While it all goes, still
there is sequence: the School of Storytellers
    was the first to disappear.

16   "Tell me, Jung-chi",
asked Dame Macleod in her West Sea castle,
    "Is God naturally good?"
"No madam no more than a wolf".
She in a low voice: "This is worse than Swift".

17   *"L'homme qui médite est un animal dépravé"*.
Vera Figner studied medicine in Zurich,
returned to Russia and agitated,
was run out of her practice, and steeled herself
to serve as one of the Judiths

18   who offered up the Czar Alexander. Back
from the casino, Dostoyevsky had stared
into his mirror and shuddered.
On Kant's wall, Rousseau,
"the Newton of morals".

19   Through a midnight street
under a sun umbrella, a cyclist
straight down the center,
between bolted villas
trailing his signboard: VOTE

20   Herr Hadlob, Minnesinger and
    migrating goose,
were you distressed when Herr Bismarck made off
with your hand-painted book? The bullfinch pecks at your sill
    and I doff my hat to you.

21   Gunning it in neutral,
the trucker hauling away
tons of newsprint –
everyone must have "views" –
fumes while the blind man crosses.

22 We live
    with our own hells
    about as long
    as the fly lights
    on a burning light bulb.

23 A mother pointing to the ant
    knows her boy may
    or may not crush it, and waits.
    Gnomon, finger in sun,
    in the firestorm love's index.

24 Here Hegel eased his Geist.
    Here Joyce and Musil, neighbors, never met.
    Here Mann climbed Pisgah.
    Here Canetti learned to love cities.
    Hier Heidi war geboren.

25 We are not here to judge.
    And so there is the American author
    lurching through alcoholic slush onto tram tracks
    CLANGCLANG whom I yanked back into literature.
    "F--k 'em!" fist flailing, "'Nam again!"

26 From one year to the next Charles Péguy
    in the stall for thrown-off books
    in the Minster's ballistic shadow –
    "The church can never reopen the workplace without paying the
        price of economic revolution for eternal salvation" –
    for which the scholar laid out 720 *petits sous*.

27 Here Heidegger dragged out his seminar.
    Here Wagner conducted his affairs.
    Here Steffi Geyer brought the strings that untuned Bartók.
    Here Max Ernst scuttled seriousness.
    Hier Ulysses war geboren.

28 "The Gold Card? But anyone
    can get a Gold Card.
    Mine, mine is Platinum.
    The Platinum Card
    is a matter of divine election".

29　　　Scratched out
　　　on the billboard, the eyes
　　　　of the fashion model.

30　Bourgeois marriage's last hymn
　　was inscribed by Beethoven.
　　Must one lack a thing to praise it?
　　At the eaves, five knobbly-necked sparrows,
　　future Leonoras, challenge the violins.

31　From the high oriel window
　　　　of an alley
　　at sacrosanct midnight,
　　the fluid madness of a ballade
　　　　by Chopin.

32　Russians on forced marches
　　to outflank Buonaparte,
　　and the Polish draftees straggled,
　　lugging their twelve-foot Madonna:
　　"Let's just stay here at Rapperswil".

33　In the lake castle, glass cases
　　with blurry linoleum-block
　　money from Solidarnòsc
　　and plaster casts of Frédéric
　　Chopin's hands.

34　"Nothing means more to me
　　than the Italian resistance!"
　　but Silone stared in disbelief
　　at his future wife:
　　an Irish spy for OVRA?

35　　　Roar of the fighter
　　"star web on the sword-sheathing lake"
　　　　trailing the sight of it
　　while a noose flies over the piling
　　and paddle wheels flailingly reverse.

36 Girl in braids and a pastor,
a Persian and his mother,
officers on the deck
as the wing formation goes over
"Look up and are not fed".

37 To the wide bow wave
a gull flies closer, a turtle
bequeathes bubbles.

38 Sturdy, hearty appearance,
children and old ones gazing
into the hotly glistening
pit of red pistons, brass valves, as
the big ship takes them away.

39 Ugo Foscolo fled Buonaparte
and came to live with the chickens
in a vicar's backyard
in Protestant Hottingen.
"Send me my Dante".

40 Foscolo fled Zurich for London
where he bought a garden cottage
but declined to teach Italian
to the ladies. "Send money,
in this country it is a sin to be poor".

41 If a man's illegitimate daughter
becomes his housekeeper, then
Mnemosyne looks kindly on him.
Foscolo's commentary on Dante
in the misprinted English version

42 netted him four pounds a week,
but then there were the creditors,
and the roof leaked on the *Inferno*.
Pastoral Zurich! Six lines of Homer a day,
boiled meat, and stinking soup.

43 Polytonal Furtwängler
    at Berlin's end in Switzerland
    fine-tuning a radio:
    "They say X is dead, and Y,
    but where is the one I'm waiting for!"

44 Inside the bookshop window
    the local product lay wrapped
    in prefaces by Sontag.
    The scholar stared: "I have not
    fled far enough".

45 Haughty rider on the road
    from Baden to Sankt Gallen
    is a papal secretary
    with a fine finger for scrolls
    rotting in monks' privies,

46 thus Poggio toting a Quintillian
    in his saddle bags,
    leaf shadow in his sleep,
    and on his tongue phrases

47 about muslin shifts on the women
    wading into the baths.
    And when they burned
    John of Prague in Konstanz
    he raged and wept.

48 Alpine self-interview
    on a terminal moraine
    among Fallen Erratics
    in voce profondo?
    Goes without saying.

49 Merry music of street work:
    flame-hissing mouth, then spewed stone
    and tar, then pouding steel –
    O animula, parvula,
    how to make your way.

50   The rippled pianola of Liszt
and stage melodramatics filled the first flics.
    Old wine! And still
when the waiter uncorks a classic bit of cellarage
the customer narrows his eyes with pleasure.

50A   And this is not my pleasure.
"I watered my horse in cavities of the Wall".
Fire's cool void in the fingers, wind's flame in the gaze.
A mess of still pools, slavery drawing down, ditch and shovel.

51   Back in my province
a flag hung out of the window
    signified a sermon,
a moral fluttering in the drafts of paradox.
This city too preaches and preaches.

52   The apache has his poetry
in Baudelaire's Paris, Apollinaire's New York,
while the fleeing jongleur of Zurich
refurbishes the gait of the ragpicker.

53   Mist rubs a hole in the mountain, loopholes
    siphon value to the vaults,
Baudelaire boasts about shoes plugged with paper,
and the console-wired graphomaniac adds zeroes
    to the sliding sum.

54   Let us praise Archilochus,
Old Testament of the Id.
"If you can't f--k it, and
you can't sell it, and
it ain't Greek, kill it".

55   Let us compose our variations
upon Goethe's satisfied epigrams.
"In the coolness after phantom
lovemaking, out of the power that blooded
your thing, you make some other thing..."

55A   Ditch and shovel, still pools down the tunnel,
fire-voided fingers, flame-rippled gaze,
and this is not my pleasure.
"I watered my horse in cavities of the Wall".

56   In the tool shed
the shovel wobbles, indoors
the lampshade:
young metals of the mountain are speaking
to the coat hangers of the heart.

57   "Here Wrng Wei hangs up his wooden hay rake,
and his round-sided ladder,
and the brace for his spine,
and incense in perpetuity
to Sung-lin, Nurse of Peasants".

58   The Bank Habib
has abolished fixed interest.
Brochures from the Bank Habib
are piled up in Zurich
every Sunday and burnt.

59   Teacher swings
a laughing malformed child
around the street corner,
redbird sinks through branches
to the clamorous nest.

60   Stone arch over the torrent,
Romanesque chapel,
quarry in the hills
over the stone museum, and the wheezing
attendant with stone lung.

60A   Fire's cool gaze fingering the void, inflaming
the tunnel mouth, a fusilade over pooled ditches
so that "I watered my horse in cavities of the Wall"
and this is not my pleasure.

61 Orange raincoat,
    blue hat, black river of hair,
    white gloves knifing up,
    and a queen's ankles
    separate fast traffic.

62   A bent alpine farmer
    piles stones from his meadow into cairns
        along the hairline paths.

63 "You are not inclinded
    to survey the visibilities
    of Zurich and its adjacencies?
    Mais, Monsieur Lenin,
    have you not come here on an annuity?"

64   The cement basement
    of the Muse's house: puffing steam pipe on a wall,
        irked visitors searching for "works".

65   Fuming steam pipe
    on a relentless wall, patrons of the Muse
        lodging protests.

66 The nuclear engineer sojourned
    seven months in an ashram.
    From his ring grinned and waved the guru.
    "If you are lucky he will
    materialize one for you".

67   Is it any worse, this
    stink of state rockets on a holiday,
        any hollower than
    the snap and ripple of massed banners?
    What I have mislaid is

68 the wet light under mushrooms, the sound
    of streams far under a plank bridge,
        the transparency
    of the wing that has just passed and
        flashed before the beginning.

69   A sikh clasped his white-muslined companion
     in the rushes, his temple
     burning behind him,
     while a green light
     blinked on and off at the landing.

70   "What We Are Fighting For":
     a pope gesturing benediction
     while dropping his penny
     in the Red Cross cannister,
     followed by a Swiss general.

71   The Wheel of Fortune
     is a roulette disc.
     Voltaire is a bloodied bust
     inscribed *Candide*. And a canny
     Ghandi waits in the wings.

72   Candidly Kokoschka painted it
     in London in 'forty-three.
     By 'eighty-three the flood had beached it
     at the Kunsthaus. Thus the Sheik's doll
     glances at it in passing.

72A Boats at their June moorings slapping companionably,
     muteswans dipping their necks singly or in pairs,
     belling their wings out to dry while peonies and the Tree Rose
     vie for evening honors, magenta against blood purple,
     early summer in the ripples, antiquity quickening in the moon,
     swans resuming their patrols, singly or in pairs, the Tree Rose
     open long into the short nights and the cool hours.

73   Met a frog
            at the bank:
         gulped, blinked, and squatted down.

74   Saw a frog
            among the swans:
         looked the other way.

75 *Brek yo nek,*
    advised a frog in the forest.
        I slowed my pace.

76 In white coats
    bent over black holes, over proteins
    and the brain's Mariana Trench,
        ears pressed
    against matter and the scrolls of the Vedas –

77 while sun imprints
    the lintel of a hut near the high pass,
        route of armies
    and strangers: *God save us
    from Storm, from Avalanche, and from Terror.*

78 Frog chirp is, but no Four Legs,
    dawn reflects in the pond
    where no sun burns, no water spreads,
    and the path curves up from shoreline
        with no walker.

79 Raw and ancient April,
    the baby warbler repeats
    his instilled melody.
    "Returning with the years",
    everything at stake.

80 Bird tune beating the leaves,
    wind beating at the pane,
    moon beating on the yard.
    Dr Johnson clung to each, trying
    not to lose his mind.

81 Imlac gestured broadly
    from the roof of the Burghölzli.
    "For five years I have restrained
    the rage of the dog star, and mitigated
    the fervours of the crab".

82 In forty years
    the tempo of Beethoven has slowed
        by one third
    while semiconductors, encoding a fat *Logic* and a Psalm,
    draw from them one tone untwisting among overtones.

83 Thus the language of the world
    hums alongside the speech of the sage,
    a whipped top that rescues
    gravity into dance,
    no loves, no quarrels, no deals.

84 Thus in poised lucubration
    behind shut eyes, thinking whirls
    to the annulment of massy thoughts,
    as all anew weightlessly attend
    to the History of the Prince of Abissinia.

85 Shadowfoot, king
    among the one-leggèd,
    sallies forth like a sprinter,
    and on a July scorcher
    kicks up his sunshade.

86 Hail, speedy Shadefeet!
    Isidore's praises
    and Aristophanes'
    merit rehabilitation.
    And lend us now your cover.

87 No mystery at all
    about the former legionaire
    pinching soup cans into a biker's helmet
    under the lantern jaw of Savonarola.
    That is Richard Savage.

88 And the fellow bowing vibratoes
    on an abstract violin
    while two Guest Workers smash up café tables
    as the girl watches?
    Rameau's nephew.

88A   Three tailored American blacks in predawn darkness
         ranged through a hotel courtyard
       like a team deprived of its hoop while the hotelier watched
         from his stone porch, plump and bored.

89   Bottled waters promise island holidays.
       Blue moons envisage cheese and surf.
       But where has that man
       gone with his lantern, looking for man?

89A   Through a streetlamp's cone mist streaming as one turned:
                                                    HEY MAN
         HOW DO WE GET OUTTA HERE!
         and he blessed them with his RAUS! and a stubby
         skyward forefinger

90   Come scratch my back,
       blackbird, as when I left
       your island brother and came here.
       Bring my scrolls, and bring
       that green sea of leaves.

90A   While Neptune on his greasy wall fountain slid to the tune
         of dribbled plashings,
         forking trash aside from his foam-spewing thoroughbred,
         that beachhead a tidied crashing.

91   Ten years ago
       with alpenstock roaming these tables
           the last man from his valley
       to speak that dialect, stalking the wedding guest
       under the iron sign of the peacock's tail.

92   In the morning
       setting the bedbugs
       on fresh paper in sunlight,
       at evening
       replacing them in the cot.

93 The Writers' Association
    got a German Jewess deported
    back to the Führer: she published
    without getting her green paper. So who says
    that free expression is meaningless?

94 Two men in their fifties
    striding side by side,
    yes! identical twins,
    growlly, all business,
    each talking to himself.

95 The tank-like wren
    hops, gobbles,
    then delivers himself
    of interviews on the ever-
    present crisis.

96 Will no one listen
    to the swollen marsh tit?
    His grandfather was a pastor
    and his cousin has reformulated
    the global organization of production.

97 Testing air-raid sirens
    as the watchmaker
    closes for lunch
    and the fruit seller
    resorts his peaches.

98 Danton roars in the sleep
    of Monsieur Lenin
    next door to young Büchner's walk-up
    via Wells's time machine:
    the decay of rhetoric.

99 Aquinas at the gate of the end
    fell silent. But then there is
    The Customs Inspector: "Mr Lao Tzu,
    if that's what you've got in there, then
    put it all down on paper".

100   And so Frisch read Brecht's exile poem
      on how the *Tao Te Ching* came to be,
      from a windflapped carbon
      while standing in the street:
      'Copy and pass it on'.

101   Here Walser was a houseboy.
      Here Walser clerked in a bank.
      Here Walser clerked insurance.
      Here Walser addressed envelopes
      in a *Stube* for the jobless.

102   Grey doric columns
      carrying red carved beams
      carrying the green vine
      into ramparts, pasture, cloud.

103   Here Walser clerked at a long table
      in a sewing-machine factory.
      Here Walser set out on fleet foot
      for a factory in Winterthur,
      where he stretched elastics.

104   A Christmas evening graveyard
      sheltered by mountains from the wind:
           hundreds of cupped red candles.

105   In the ancient barn, canned music
      for pigs who never see daylight,
      on Hanged Man Pine Tree Road.
      So once there grew a harsh light, where now
      dark meat fattens for the dark-minded.

106   The lady offers to buy them
      both a cup of coffee.
      Seated, she says, "I'm hungry!"
      The scholar pays for both platters. She:
      "Next time I'll tell you about my socialism!"

107   Walser to Lenin
      in Spiegelgasse: "Do you also enjoy eating
           this Glarner Birnbrot?"

108   The headlines part to disclose
      Yevtuschenko in folksy shirt
      premiering his filmy childhood in Venice
      ("Eternal Venice sinking by degrees
      Into the very water that she lights").

109   The sidewalk spritzer advances, twelve
            nozzles sizzle,
      order drips in their wake,
      while the plastic reservoir sloshes
            seas, chaoses.

110   (Mark it well, managers and soaks,
      cheats and charitables, you wise
      savers and reckless go-for-brokes,
      whether it came or went: it dies.

111   And whether you hoard your thin life,
      Midas, or richly squander it,
      Duke of Chin, or cannot get enough,
      Faustus, death writes the final chit.)

112   "Space is not what they say,
      and then there is *le Mouvement*..."
            Oscar Milosz
      threading a cowbell angelus among
            mists on the Rigi.

113   No Roman death mask of Brecht
      over the Bechstein grand
      polished by late sun
      high on the Zurichberg.

114   A muteswan heaved itself up onto the quai,
      rolling and unrolling its neck, galoshes
      slapping over the stones. *Clackclack* went its bill above
      the birdbook, wing stroke enough to break an arm.

118   Nearsighted scholar and messenger of heaven
      gazed at each other for a long moment
      in Orwell's target year, the Year of the Rat. Winter fogs,
      and "in *The Spring and Autumn* there are no righteous wars".

116   The street musician shrugs and packs it in:
      two whores grin down
      from their breasty window,
      radio still blaring.

117   August heat, night window wide,
      the world breathing where
      a man under a lamp near his radio
      sits naked to the waist,
      his arm timing late Mozart.

118   "We filed out of the woods" (militia)
      "and there in the meadow, a hut
      with lamps and pictures on the outside,
      the old man and goat inside.
      And the village still called him their own".

119   Having clambered to the top of his field,
      he owns a fifteenth-century house.
      A magnet hangs in the bathtub,
      another hangs in the mineral water, and the little
      clincher hangs in the orange juice.

120   Sparrow my alarm clock
      to aereate my slumbers in the house
            of Paracelsus.

121   In dialect the Frau shoos her goats
              among cowplates,
      a young intruder barks Deutsch to his
              radio-controlled jeep.

122   In the Swiss monthly
      for paraplegics, athletes
      wheelchair down a sprinting track
      among paintings of cherry pickers
      toppling out of trees.

123   On the truck flatbed, a stack
of gleaming sheetrock,
in the air the musings
of Monsieur Mallarmé
while they lift and unload:

124   *Uno*
        per
  lor-
    o,
  uno
        per
  il Signor
  Diavo-
        lo,
  e uno
        per
            noi!

125   Silone's window looked out on the mountains.
So did Brecht's window, but he was not
interested: Brecht was interested in things
that could move. And Silone's fugitives, no movement
left to them, vanish into the high snows.

126   Swansdown
    and junkies' needles
snared in the hurdles of abandoned weirs.

127   Leapers around a bonfire before
the emeryboard Opera House Extension
while masked extras beat their shields
with nightsticks in the wings.

128   Each night during the youth riots
streets were hosed and vacuumed.
So the morning shift still dozed, fathers
looked past their children, the powerful
blow of life swung wide.

129 The Roman baths have been resurrected.
But at the swimming complex designed by Frisch
workmen sliced off a hanged man at the knees,
refusing to widen the excavation
on his account.

130 Just listen to that one-man band:
unfolds like a harmonica,
opens himself like a drum hole,
and through it he goes up,
free from grief, free from snow.

131 Fleshy crosses of clematis
trellising the city mind
one mid-May moment
with country mind.

132 Lakeside restaurant:
it is napkins in floral sprays,
and a portrait photo that says
that here you'll not go in want:
it is the owner's face, and the owner-wife's, and it is Richard
Nixon's.

133 "No phosphorous, no thoughts": thank you, Doktor Professor
Moleschott.
Driving against pilings, the surge bursts into boiled cauliflower,
each cluster melting at impact, somewhat overcooked, the tailrace
a swirl of inedible disjecta. No moonlight, no phosphorous.

134 "Pine's waist thin jade now", sang Wu Wenying
  at the hetaira's grave
while a jay grieved for the tree.

135 Lake gulls follow the tractor,
settle in swirls
over fresh furrows,
but the worm startles them.

136   Startled, touching her hair, the widow
      blows a kiss to her dead
      while flowers deepen and shine
      under sudden rain, row
      on garden row.

137   Blasted to the isle of Ufenau
      by Erasmus, syphilis, and the Curia,
      Ulrich von Hutten laid down sword and pen:
      "One lives off the countryside, the forest,
      each castle keep...Haggard peasants...."

138   One sail up the lake,
      one sail down,
      one bomb in the blue, one
      in the sea, one in the ground, with our
      little sun between.

139   Perfected waves
      smoothing to nothing, teaching
          the unperfected.

140   Artemidorus and Jung-chi
      co-laborers of a morning,
      with Synge and the gull he watched
      through a long morning on Aran
      trying to break a golf ball on the rocks.

141   Only a return summer visitor
      to her wild Aran shores, you are,
      yet she sits at your knee, Psyche
      of the living tresses, to see
      the photos you brought back.

142   Hand-carried from a Nile cliff to this lake,
      the sayings set down by Judas Thomas:
      "All of them sozzled and no one thirsty, though
      they came here empty and will have to leave that way.
      Blind drunk, for the moment. But when they shake it off..."

143   Unearthed by monks at Einsiedeln,
      Mechtilde von Magdeburg's love cry:
      "I want the unmingled wine!"
      (After the ceremony they poured their best vintage,
      but most of it trickled through my beard.)

144   Halfway up the black Adlisberg
      a woodsman came down shouldering a golden log.
      He asked, "What are you doing staring at stars
      through stripped beeches in piercing December?"
      And I asked, "Why are you hauling that imponderable
      treasure down into the dead city?"
      Before we could speak further, lake mist rose and belltowers
      blinded us with four luminous strokes.

Rhyme Prose Six

When the People's Army turned against the people, it went something like this.

Dogs used to wear all the horns; stags had none. So whenever Stag fought with Goat, Goat always licked him. Stag begged the ducks to plead with the dogs to lend him their horns.

Now, the ducks knew that Stag would never give them back, so they wished him well but told him to find another middleman.

So Stag went to Rooster. Rooster hustled off, the dogs were persuaded, and back came Big Red with the equipment. Stag taught Goat a thing or two about defeat, then vanished into the forest.

So to this day Rooster cries, *Lok kah hwen konko-á* – Give the hounds back their horns! But the ducks cackle, *Hawk-awk-ah-ah-awk*, wagging their heads: We knew what that Stag was going to do!

Johannes Bobrowski was marched off by a millenium in the making, past Novgorod, where his comrades chose to spill the cloister bells into snow. Past villages in the north, "no one will learn where we were," the better to retain the lineaments of Sarmatia. Óndra Lysohorsky took shelter in Tashkent-Kuibyshev, then in Moscow. His nation, younger than he was, had been crushed back to the peoples who must send forth both raven and dove. Qu Qiubai, nation-hunting, went to fledgling Moscow, by way of rotting in Harbin, hallucinating enlightenment in the Manchurian boondocks. A Czech and a *nabi* from Shanghai converging on some hidden territory perhaps of most ancient name perhaps stretching new boundaries. Bobrowski found in certain plain words a hidden territory nearly, ah nearly impervious to the long guilt of the raven. This he hid beneath his wing, this he carried towards Sarmatia. Lu Xun did not move; Lu Xun scoured bricks with acid as the new walls went up around him, perhaps to the good, yet remind us, Boethius, that in your cell you fingered no rosary, but rather the rational beads of *amor quo caelum regitur*. In the end Lu Xun had to dispatch Lao Tzu through the last outpost again, into the blown wastes of the northwest, having him tell the guards, "The nameable names are not the names that name permanence." And the copyist dozed, his brushes cascading to the floor. Qu Qiubai made it back to Shanghai, electing the mystique of foundry sweat. By the osprey he was devoured. Łysohorsky returned to his Latchik miners, saving for them and their children the ikon of Saint Francis. Him the fledgling hawk lashed with its steel beak. Bobrowski was demobbed into moldering internment, along with his Christ of Memory, and Proserpinal psalms brewed from a second Buonaparte's muddy folly, their *Selah* breathing out ever the word "bird", and a map he was refining with the aid of that bird's eye, a map of Sarmatia.

Dear friend, from this window
the path to the end is clumped violets
turning sun into moist lobes
that exhale the undersea and night past Arcturus.
The black mirror stays real.
But enduring it, good hands
make gardens.
                Where
the arbor ladders shade
floats a stair, sliding if you gaze at it,
and that is the ascent, old friend:
our climb, the stink of it
with the weariness, burning ledges
contoured to each corrugation
of those ephemeral
radiant leaves.

Hill Country Ballad

    Bowee, boweree,
went through this gate in a high year, but remember
clearly only the great weight falling away,
    bowee, bowdowneree,
as bass at evening flash over brazed water.

    Bowee, boweree, bowee,
lies of the time and my part in them, inertly
manifest in these crystallographies,
    bowdowneree,
part of the crucible's intricate walled peace,

    bowee, boweree,
where snare drum riffs among the pumpkin lanterns
bobbing on sticks as children to the clock tower
    bowee,
cleanse the slow lattice of each interlock,

    bowee, boweree,
but the rash return, devout feet memoryless
troll me to my knees, hands cupped in amber,
    bowdowneree,
and the fresh catch torn living from my side.

The Cells at Tun-huang

Where now hangs the saddlebag of pointless zeal for Yen Hui,
where lies the road to dark Wei and its dictator?

Where has it blown, the sandtrack to dissipated Emirs
for barefoot Francis, where the fire that englobed him?

Where are they, the left hands of Mucius Scaevola, charred,
and of Colonel von Stauffenberg, mangled but willing?

Where scrapes the trench shovel of Musonius Rufus,
where rock the lever and treadle of Simone Weil's drill press?

Where is it shelved, the parchment of first entitlement,
and where has he gone, the man who recognized it, reading its blanks?

"Then who is it standing before me!" bawled the emperor.
"I cannot tell you!" barked the wayfarer, and walked off.

Into grey mosses bearding a blue cliff.
Into the blessing before battle, in the mass sung raggedly afterwards.
Cursèd be he / they / we! This too shall pass, but not adroitly.
In the psalms of the man pulled from flood by a stag, and therefore
in the emperor's lust for the stag, that his horns be turned into wine cups,
in the saved one's betrayal of the deer to the throne-holder,
in the eavesdropping swallow's flight, for he told all in time, and in
the stag's rebuke to the emperor, for this in turn
made the wretch confess to his ruler, who demanded:
"Shudderer, stutterer, where is the golden one who spoke here,
where has he gone, who gave you your useless redemption?"

Into the air past your portals, O great one,
not the air but the earth stretching away, magnificence,

not the wide but the red earth, high one, reddened
to cochineal by petals of the mango, eminence,

where they have fallen, majesty, and blooded our ground,
there one may pursue him, the foregoer, the horned knower.

Tail of the Magpie

Swan lumbering south at dawn,
    mated grebes knitting ripples,
goose preening on the seawall, mudhens
    plunging, mallards
        wheeling raggedly –

heron from the landing
    as mist lifts, lifting away,
the blue gravel barge at noon
    plowing empty to Rapperswil,
a goldeneye dipping its umber head
    for crumbs tossed onto the moon's track:

stay, servants of appetite,
sentinels of these hours.

Centaurs and centurions

. . .

Centaurs? Centurions?

– Vítězslav Nezval, c.1938

Folksong II.xii of the Classic Anthology

In the lowland there
a dead deer
mantled in white grasses,
madness in a woman in springtime
favors lovers.

Where elm shoots
straggle at the wood's edge,
white sedges
over jade laid away, find
the doe lying.

Hey! take your hand
off my sash!
But wait, stay –
stay, or you will set
the dog barking.

Honan Folksong

(sung to two-string violin and wooden-plate drum)

Uphill and down and again uphill,
he takes hill after hill
and will never get his fill,
upridge and down and again upridge,
he takes ridge after ridge
and high edge piled on high edge.
It lines out and winds on,
the venerable, improbable
vine of the araconda,
and the hesitant pheasant
shoos off in a tattoo that his long
tail flails *whang whang* –
a big python writhes on the path,
with a sliding push to the bush
slithering thither

and singing honky-tonk
   the apprentice monkeys
   go go go up the pine trunk
and everywhere the invisible note
   of swelling elegy from the nigh-
   tingale's yellow throat,
where all you see is
   cloud and more cloud
   and mist swirling past,
mountains a whiteness
   and whiteness where the lines
   of the pines were:
hid in that wood
   a temple, and in that temple hid
   a lone man and good.

from *Folksong I.ix of the Greater Odes, the Classic Anthology*

Gong and drum boom,
stone and flute tones hang clear,
and in good grain there is ringing,
let clanging ears of it come.

Real work pays off. Our empty
cups have filled us with wine,
fortune forever greens
and returns with new grain.

Mencius VI.1.viii

Where the cypresses of Ox Mountain lie axed
        the rains bathe them,
    shoots sprouting from stumps –
but each day the cows come
        to nuzzle them clean:
the Ox lies stripped bare
        by his brides, even –
yet in the windless forerising
        day buds from darkness:
let the pale tips
        answer to mists now and dew,
let great Ox stir through his felled shanks
        and green dawn over him.

Single Seal Quodlibets

    Rooftile and shield rim:
        shielding the house
    and roofing the warrior,
        two seasons of shelter
    over one head surviving neither.

        Stagecoach footstrap
    easing me down out of battle
    to approach with measured step
    the cleared space, steadier
        in my grip
    on the outstretched bowl
        held low, held level.

    To begin is to make offering,
       take, present it
    lifted up, be lifted and so
    raise the bowl and begin –
    saying it is furthering it:
    to further it, say it by moving it
       along, get it en route –

that is the whole record, the all
   if you take the bowl and begin:
          give out the lifting up
   and be lifted in the bowl of the beginning,
   for that making is a way-making
          in the bowl so taken,
   the beginning cupped in and raised up:
          presentation.

   Pavanne before the Winter Campaign

          Speech of the sky, wide cloud
   from its house streaming unbroken –
          your passing has stripped the beds
   of every rose, has uprooted
          the spirit.

   Time now to stoke the kilns, rack gourds for firing,
   mound charcoal and bisque the soft flasks,
   time to smooth tight the shroud collar, and the sash,
   and overlay the coverlet, and bear it down to the pit –
   stretch wet mallow in your traps, snug as a lute strap,
   for a black song lifts past the river's high shore

          sky loud
          streaming
   north face of Shadow Mountain
   intervalled mist
          fevery rose
   with the face of the friend
          rooted
   wine from wattle shoots
          spir

          So now for pan pipes
   fluting the midyear sacrifice,
   cool trill pulling the river clear,
          unmuddying the heart:
   deep shine sliding out
          into the rites of summer.

Two and Three Seal Medley

The river is the law

even though you are bound to your land
as the comet is wound around its orbit

And of course if you drain the marshes between mountains
and lug lead from the mines at Yen
and float it on scows to the south
the river is the law

And then, too, if your door
feathers itself in fire,
if the wing of the flame bird marks your passage
and your wicker threshold is for burning
law is the river

Law may be the measure
for measure is the fire
renewing and furthering
the heat and sweat of the job
such, surely, has been the law

and a man standing
straight and unblinking in his rank
may well be the lance shaft of the law

but even so and ever
law is the river

Chou Medley

Turmoil
    in the fabric,
hands at the skein
    unweaving:

tumult,
>   white water at the ford,
splash of the finale –
may the cadenza
>   smooth it again.

Moan over Chou!
>   Caw it out, slow.

Lean times, hard times,
calamities to keep off –
to be rich? not enough,
>   nor to be pious.

Harsh times breeding fear,
>   fire over Chou –
devils to expel,
>   poisons to bleed –
>   fat meats to spread
on the shore, offering them to the swell.

>   Jug abuzz
with a baby wasp,
Sam Walker's jug.

Fast feather
sent
from a pheasant –
and from the oak's
gladness
vast push
below, above
vast reach.

Journey's end and work done,
>   this place detains us,
our settlement – and thus
we have come into line,
block drums under the mallet's tune.

Age of Gold

The huddled egg breaks open,
new leaves move on the tree
      for Lord Lucky –
   his cup runneth over
bearing out the big-bowl reading of happiness

...*but let us rerun that sequence*:
      blind trust
beaks through the warm shell
   while fear trembles the tree –
      for Lord Lucky
a claw slices down
      beside the hand
cupped around his child.

Of what use plunder
   to prisoners of war?
Hemp dangling fruit by the outworks.
Across a wide famine
    birdcatchers
   drag at the wind,
men try drumming
   bream to the surface,
their rafts adrift on a fast current, O Lord
     Lucky!

        Mayflies
thronging the air.

Barometric Reading Incorporating Single Graphs

   Remembering
      has gone the way of soft speaking
  yet much chatter animates
     the Lucretian quanta of danger –

    garrulous
        cliff after cliff,
and a wind like three dogs barking
    or a dog coming down
like a wind with three toothed howls in it –

a loop of furry risk.

But in the pauses of it,
    grain hushing,
wheat standing quiet.

Western Palace Rhapsodies

(from Single-Seal Readings of Oracle Bones)

    Flock on flock
agitated, stimulated, trying to get off the ground –
    fevers and guttering fires
and thunders ebbing, snakes wriggling in the nest,
miniscule twists all over the silkworm frames.

Family pantomimists in a row
    and a leaking roof corner.

    Pronouncements promulgated
in accents of the personal letter,
    and so the squares fill
for lay sermons in the rhythms of exorcism
promoting bearskins and the toothed capes of tigers.

Forehooves hobbled
    by the relay post,
millet fading
    by the void warden's hut,
manure drying
    over unbroadened ground –

heap up boundary stones but unbar the door,
put some metal in your mouth and get going,
    shoot your horse through the gate –

there is no visiting card to the endless spaces, and yet
    the lute shines under running winds,
    the ladle hangs among star dragons.

Liu Xie, Wenxin diaolong zhu, 6.521

Writing alters
    and therefore abides.
Braiding rope
    it makes fast to adequacy.
So go where the day leads you
    and finish what it began.
Grasp chances, grope
    through openings, fear is a phantom.
Keep your eye on the event
    and give back its strange contours,
ask the old ones: learn from them
    how laws came into being.

Lament in Wet Spring

Li Ho

How did Tza-ra
come cackling on the White Donkey
    over those razor peaks?

Irish James lies now
many years in his figured sepulchre,
    a pile of stinking bones.

And the high priest Zwing-li
has his inlay coffin of black rosewood.
What a waste of abalone.

Dawn in Shih-Cheng

Li Ho

Moon is setting over Great Dike,
Lady and Herd Boy ford the high river –
where is the lane not washed by havoc, where
    is the one place?

Streaming time, the ten
cauldrons of the unborn are pouring
their northern surf as we listen for
    their boomings.

Marsh tits harry the cygnets,
I have dropped my scroll in shore eddies,
come January my labors will
    lock in the pond.

Gull after gull breaks open white day,
a girl, weeping, has turned into wing flash.
Stroke your zither no more, Nomad Boy – a bronze bell
    hangs brooding in the cloud forest.

from *Twenty-three Poems about Horses*

Li Ho

1   Dragon spine fluttering with money,
    mint-issue hooves trampling the mist white,
    but no one weaves saddle flaps of silk brocade.
    Who will cast for him a gold pizzle whip?

2   Midwinter grasses, sweet roots, and in boulevards
    of the capital snow bunches like salt.
    To see if his mouth is hard or soft
    take him in hand first with a bramble bit.

9   Shu of Liao's boy died in a hurry,
    no one any more can feed fire breathers.
    Night deepening, frost leans on the stables
    of thoroughbreds, west wind splitting their hooves.

11 A court dandy's mount given over to his lady,
    silver trappings pricked with piebald bitch unicorns –
    and at high noon above the salt cliffs
    it scrambles for footing, drained, against wind and dust.

13 Whose son is this gentleman of jade rings?
    They say a knight's bones are fragrant – sun, barley, and long time –
    and he has heaped out gold for the bones of one horse,
    setting them on the road with King Hsiang of Ch'u.

17 Iron glinting into grain still green,
    millstones dribbling grass in a fine scatter –
    today's crowd is set on narrow-necked fillies,
    and the big outfits are wary of long teeth.

18 Po-lo once looked this horse over,
    noting his credentials, hair swirls along the belly.
    Now they feed him white grass and give no interviews.
    Which sun will he leap with over Blue Mountain?

Han-shan, poem XXIV

Cold Mountain writes you this,
credences no one credits.
Honey is licked up by men
but never medicine,
easiness brings them some peace,
balked rage blows that to bits,
but just look, will you, at puppets,
laid flat by their fling on the stage.

Tung-Shan Liang-chieh

– "For whom did you strip off your finery"?
 – "One bird note herds all wanderers home".
Even with flowers gone, it will go on
  calling from woods among the peaks.

Weeping for Ying Yao

Wang Wei

Stone Tower Mountain
home to tombs
home to the tomb
we have taken
you we have taken
up the tower
the peak death
have gone with you
home
and now we
lean down
through cypress, pine
carriages and the hearse
we have set your
bones among clouds
have seen you
home
no more
never again
setting among clouds
your bones
and now
down go
carriages leaning
pine, cypress
never again
no more
what stays

are the torrents
shooting fixedly
white water
mindlessly
this is what stays
only this
stationary
spilling
tomb, tower
death the mountain
mindlessly
down to men.

Sent to Yü Te-fu on His Receiving a Commission in Chekiang on the Ch'ien t'ang

Tsung Ch'en

When Alexander dismantles his iron curtain, disclosing to you the Ten Tribes wiring olives back onto the trees taken from them by the other Two;

when your shoes trail no tissues and gums of Araby through the avenues of Manahatta;

when you see the accounts of the armamenteers melting away on slopes beneath the Mönch and the Jungfrau,

and the farmers below K'un-lun experimenting with crop rotations in the absence of directives;

when Mi-en-leh, alias Lenin, in Brecht's *Me-ti* or *Book of Twisters*, assures us with horsewhip in hand that he is actually our slave (but this has already happened),

and when Confucius in Pound's *Unwobbling Pivot* – "Everyone eats and drinks, few can distinguish the flavors" – adds in his table talk: "The proper man is not a dish" (but this, too, has occurred), that is, when finally the two of them, with their pair of promoters, converge on a bridge and have merry palaver,

and when MacDiarmid joins them and collars them into following him to a meadow where he barks at the stones and the stones rise, and amble whitely, and begin to bite the herb;

when reports in the liberal weeklies proceed verbatim rather than through mangled paraphrase,

and do not take credit for "promising developments" at the back of the North Wind, at the roots of avalanches, and in the misery-sloshing tides of realignment,

then you'll know: you have crossed over Red Pine's deathless threshold.

Wang Yang-ming

Emptiness at ease is not the great void,
brewing within it, a balancing stirred in the first mortar.
What does it hold
              lacking which we are at lack?

When high feeling has passed, air clears to the last ground.
Action inheres nowhere in remembering or refraining.
Flawless, the hiddenness of metamorphosis –
and who else will pursue it with me, if not you?

The Proem (opening)

Parmenides

The mares pulling me with such force kept on thrusting
as far as my soul could go, once the women at the reins
had gotten me on the way that the Goddess lays out,
road of seething mind tracked through speech and story,
that carries the undeflectable man on course, aiming
his thought straight. This was carrying me at last,
I could see those horses of unmappable mind
tearing along it, straining, steered by those women.
The hubs of the wheels shot fire and shrilled the pipe's high pitch,
spun forward on both sides by the whirling metal
which those priestesses, daughters of the sun,
shoot into motion when they leave the hall of night,
as they did with me, and, throwing their scarves
back over their streaming heads, make for the light.

Iliad V.837-9, Athene and Diomedes

Homer

And now the oak axle of the war chariot grated loudly
under the weight of a grim goddess and a great man.

from *Hymn V*

Callimachus

Just now I heard the whinnying of the mares
    being yoked for Pallas –
hurry, she will come any moment now....

No perfumes, no mirrors
    for our goddess,
but hurry, I hear the axles grating....

Orphic Fragment

Close to the dwelling of the dead,
           on the left you will find a spring.
Near it towers a white cypress.
Avoid that source, do not
           even try to approach it.
It is the other spring that you need, surging
from the lake of Mnemosyne,
           a cold torrent.

Before it stand guardians. Tell them,
"I am the child of earth
           and the starry regions,
but heaven is my home.
           You know that already.
Thirst burns in me,
           I am dying from it.
Let me taste the coldness
           gushing from the lake of Mnemosyne".

And they will let you drink
           from the divine source,
and you will come into dominion
           among the heroes.

Epitaph for Albert Bertschy

(Euschalpass, Canton Fribourg)

Wait, wanderer,
remember death's nearness.
In my bloom
I, a blunderer
through this garden of Edelweiss,
met my doom.

Christian Epigram, Palatine Anthology L.59

> Egyptian woman,
> hidden infant,
> and close river –
> these are the human
> earthly current
> in the Pattern-Giver,
> see it who can.

from *Poem on Divine Providence*

Orientius

The bulk of these years is already gone out of mind
    because your page is inscribed with no verses.
What conditions have made such silence your product,
    what anguish has squatted on your glum genius?

. . .

If the wide sea were to rip broadside into Gaul,
    surging toweringly across its tillage, surely
there is no beast of the field, no grain or fruit or olive
    and no choice place that would not turn rotten;
no plantations and great houses that would not be swept
    by storm crash and fire blast and be left standing blank and sad:
like shouldering a landslide, going through this ten-year slaughter
    strewn by the steel of the Vandals and Visigoths.

. . .

And then, too, you trudged among the wagons, eating dust,
    lugging weapons for the Goths, and no small bit of baggage,
beside a white-haired commoner, ruddy with the dust of cities,
    driven the same way a shepherd goads banished sheep.

. . .

So you cry over farms laid waste, courtyards deserted,
    and the flame-swept stage scenery of the villas.
How, then, not weep over losses that are truly yours,
    if you could peer into the trampled sanctums
of your heart, their splendors crudded with filth,
    and hobnailed swaggerers in the mind's cramped cell?

"Inten bec"

anonymous Irish

From the bright tip
of his bill,
his bony little
lip all yellow,
he sang it,
the little bird:
he spoke
one note of it
over the grey loch
from the cover
of a heaped branch
all yellow:
a blackbird.

Walahfrid Strabo

What enwombed the marrow now nurses a tree,
    a shin bone flowers – surely a good omen.
Amazing: the bark is not spongey, it's even
    tougher than the wood: such is the life in this bone.
Nothing, great king, shuns your service: you hunt the doe
    and a forest sprouts from her bones! Hail!

Travellers to Broceliande

This is the Book of thy descent:
this is the Book of the Grail.
Here begin the terrors,
here begin the marvels.
I, Ignavus, saw
from the middle of my hut
that book smaller than a hand
come from the hand of Christ,
come into the middle of my doubting
on the eve of Good Friday,
a heath in white Britain
holding us, that was in seven seventeen
and the book was lost, then found again...
I, J. Bodmer, saw
in the moldering pile *Parzival*,
here begins Wolfram
in the blackness of print, Zurich,
seventeen fifty-three...
But when on the third day he wished
to read more from the little book,
It had gone. "Off to Norway,
the weird beast will lead you,
you must sweat and stink": and so
past a foul hermit and black fir,
battle tower, queen's lake, convent
and a fight to the end with devils
possessing a man of God, there came
to hand the little book
and so I have set it down here
on cloudy stone, on mists
shifting through the trees.
I, Wace, historian,
wonder-hunting, bagged nothing,
came back as I went, a fool,
yes, departed a fool and came back one!
It was damn foolishness I went looking for, and
    a damn fool is what I discovered.
I, Cologrenaunt, knight errant,
Chrétien's man, saw
the chapel spring boiling ice cold

by the pillar of emerald.
Grabbed the gold basin and splashed
that water over the pillar –
the sky blackened, flashes
fell with snow, rain, hail, trees...
but then calm, and in the vine
birds thick on every branch,
each with its own song making one music
that held me contented there. Fool!
A knight barreled down on me,
a roaring giant, ripped me
off my mount, flattened me,
stole my horse, didn't even look back.
I dragged off to my host,
but they all said no one ever
got out of that scrape before.
Exactly as I left, so I returned –
now that it is over
I see my foolishness.
And exactly like a fool
I have confessed to you
what I never wanted to tell any man.

On an Almond Tree in Hungary

Janus Pannonius

What Herakles never saw
        in the Garden of the Hesperides
nor the lord of Ithaka
        on the Phaiakis of Alkinoös,
and which stirs wonder
        even where fields flourish
let alone in Hungary
        where the sun won't melt;
in grim winter, yet,
        to see an almond
daring to flower
        when frosts kill off the buds –

    you should hold out, Phyllis,
            for the force that lets Prokne
    blossom again: or
            has Demophoön
    made you hate even
            that kind of delay?

Gouty Brigit: Epigram I.284

Janus Pannonius

Gouty Brigit lying in soft grass
            and a snake creeping
towards stricken feet.
Seeing its coils, she leaped
            from her blankets running,
painlessly doctoring
the malady medicine could not touch –
whether fear did it
            or the limbs themselves,
aid came from the Macedonian beast.
How rarely the meritorious
            get their reward!
The serpent-helper was clubbed to death.
In my judgment, bitch,
            it were far better
had you changed places with your benefactor.

My Country Weeps: 1636

Andreas Gryphius

We are finished, yet still
                they have not finished with us.
Brazen troops of nations,
                crazed trumpets,
blood-slick sword
                and the big howitzer
have devoured everything that sweat
                and diligence laid away.
Towers flicker, the cathedral
                lies roof through floor,
city hall sits in terror,
                our forces smashed,
girls defiled,
                and wherever we turn
flames, plague, and mortality
                pierce heart and spirit.
Trench and street are the constantly
                refreshed conduits of blood.
For eighteen years now
                our rivers have
brimmed with corpses, slowly
                pushing themselves clear.
Yet still I have said nothing
                of what vexes like death
and dips a lashing beak deeper
                than hunger, pest, and holocaust:
that so much treasure has been
                plundered from our souls.

Goethemathy

> *A whole heap of crockery lay under the windows.*
> *A heap of broken dishes.*
>   *The demolitionist was Johann Wolfgang von Goethe,*
> *three-and-a-half years old; he had broken every*
> *dish in the house.*
> – Mandelshtam, "Goethe's
Youth: Radiodrama"

> Cottage cheese you splat
> with your boot won't get strong, just flat.

Self-born, self-made, autodidactical –
so that's your style, soul blind all along!
Come, give it a try! Since you're so practical,
you'll see, once you're peeved, how everything goes wrong.

> Sweet freedom of the TV press!
> We're finally happy-O!
> It bounces through the marketplace
> *in dulci jubilo.*

What have I got to do with church history?
No more than some priest can I see through that mystery.
How things are standing with Christians in general
certainly won't be appearing to me at all.

> Father! Father! Don't let go!
> The Erl King hurt me, hurt me so!

Admit it, poets of the West:
those Eastern poets have been the best.
But in one thing we're giants, they're elves –
the art of despising ourselves.

> Waves in plashes
> always spreading
> so the flow is
> always heading
> for the rim, and fine fat splashes
> surge from the tub and slop below.

All on their own this divine couple made their queer marriage:
Psyche turns senior and clever, Amor remains a child.

> Today at the tavern, early,
> a really gorgeous brawl –
> bartender, serving girl,
> torches, a mob! All surly,
> the flute shrilling and the drum rattling...
> pandemonium,
> but I was in there battling
> with the best of them.
>
> No question, being such a lout
> doesn't increase my moral stature.
> But I'm smart enough to stay out
> of fights the others pick with teacher.

Every fanatic should be crucified when he turns thirty,
    so the world hears of him at least once, and trick meets trickster.

> Disturb me: that's what you want to do?
> Leave me with my jug of wine!
> In company one learns a thing or two,
> but a man gets inspired alone.

How does nature manage to bridge the heights and depths
    in humanity? She sets vanity between them.

> Broom, broom,
> back in your corner!
> It's all over.
> You can zoom
> around like a demon, doing such things,
> only at your master's bidding.

I'll tell you all the strangest thing –
just think: Abraxas is what I bring.

A seal ring's hard to carve – so much
meaning's in that crannied spot –
here, surely, purity's what you touch:
the word stays buried, you hardly give it a thought.

> What wine
> got Alexander drunk?
> I'll bet you my last bit of spunk
> it wasn't as good as mine.

On those spring days, such powers...
out on the water and deep in those bowers
drinking happily and writing in a big
way indeed, bowl on bowl, swig after swig.

> A little circle
> rounds our life,
> and generations
> enduringly
> trail each other
> into existence in an
> unbroken chain.

Here it won't help to go on grooming –
they're roses, they go on blooming.

The Course of Life

Friedrich Hölderlin

You too wanted more, but love pulls us all
   downward, grief more greatly bows us down;
     yet not for nothing does our curve
         bend back to where it came from.

Upward, or down – does there not still rule
   in holy night where mute nature broods
     on futures, rule in utterly twisted
         Orcus, a straight way, a law?

That is what I found. For never, from what I know,
   have you high ones who sustain all things
     led me, as mortal masters do,
         with care by a level path.

Man shall try everything, say the high ones,
   so that, fed by strength, he may learn to give thanks
     for all, and fully grasp freedom,
        to burst through, and go, wherever.

The Tombs (conclusion)

Ugo Foscolo

*"This prophecy Merlin shall make; for I live
before his time."*
          – the Fool in *King Lear*

          Palms, cypresses,
the day will come when you'll see a blind beggar
stray through your ancient shade, feeling his way
into the tombs to take the urns in his arms
and have speech with them. Those secret vaults will moan
and the house of death will tell the whole tale,
how Troy was levelled twice and twice rebuilt
in shining splendor over silent streets
only to burnish Greek glory for the line
of Peleus taking its last prize. The poet,
easing the pain of those souls with song, will make
Greek princes deathless in every country touched
by the fathering sea. And you, Hektor, will win
the honor of tears wherever blood is held sacred
shed for one's native earth, as long as the sun
shines down on the catastrophes of mankind.

from *The Graces, Hymn I*

Ugo Foscolo

Taking pity on us in our raging
furies, all our torments, one day the holy
feminine, coming out of the white combers
she had entered to revive the herds of Nereus,
stood forth with the Graces; and the original
Ionian swell gave them welcome, the surge
that cherishes the sweet shore and its homecoming moss
and every day moves out from Cythera yearning
towards the hills that mothered me: a boy there,
I gave worship to the godhead of Venus.
My Zante! To the Veneto where brave
Antenor brought the household gods of Troy,
and where they, with my own ancestors, found
their last resting place, I give my hymns and my bones,
but I give my thoughts to you: the man who forgets
his homeland cannot speak as he should to those goddesses.

Rawlinson Two-Step

*(Poems 4 & 12, Rawlinson Ms, Bodleian, and
"Die offentlichen Verleumter", Gottfried Keller)*

*Ne sey never such a man as Jordan was;
wente he to Gogeshale panyles.*
A thief creeps out of his hole
to make his rounds, he wants
to snatch our purses, but makes
a little discovery, so now
he's after bigger game.
*Ore est temps d'alier a diner,
ore est temps d'alier a diner.
Ore alom, alom, alom,
bele companie avom.*

Arguments over nothing,
bankrupted learning,
tatters on the flagpole
over a flagging people.
Wente he to Gogeshale panyles,
ne sey never such a man as Jordan was.

Everywhere he goes
the vacuum of the times
Stondeth alle stille,
stille, stille
lets his shamelessness
puff out, and he prophesies,
climbing onto a rostrum
of stinking rubbish,
hissing his salutations
to a dumbstruck world.
Stille stondeth alle,
stille stondeth alle,
stille as any ston.

Seed hath found furrow. The earth
changes, changes. Millions
Bele companie avom
live shame and laugh at crime
ore est temps d'alier a diner
ore est temps d'alier a diner
and what had been fantasy
is now the case – the stalwart
bele companie avom
the stalwart have been scattered
and the stinkers have made their pact.

Someday, and it won't be soon,
they'll talk about these times
stondeth alle stille
as they fabulize over the Black Death,
school children muttering
through the lectionary of plagues
stille as any ston.
And the children will build in the field
a bogeyman out of stubble

to make happiness flame
from afflictions,
to torch radiance
from archaic horrors.
Trippe a littel with thy fot
ant let thy body gon.

Venus de Milo

Gottfried Keller

Once our healing nurse, now you're
reduced to being fashionable,
propped in plaster, crockery, tinware
on desktop, stove, and dressing table.

Soup bubbling, small talk's pinging fluff,
yattering brats, domestic riot –
long since accustomed to such stuff,
you show them your surpassing quiet.

How through a shining temple door
one sees you listening into far
expanses, while through the conch of your ear
the sky-blue breakers roar!

"Quand elle viendra..."

Oscar V. de L. Milosz

When she comes – will her eyes go green, grey,
grey or green in the river?
The hour will be new in that archaic future,
new, but hardly novel –
worn hours: one has seen, dreamed, spoken them all!
I pity you the knowledge...

There will be something of the day and its street sounds
just as today and always – firm ordeals –
and odors, depending on the season, September's, April's,
and the false sky, and clouds in the river;

and words, depending on the moment, spirited, broken,
under skies arranged correspondingly,
for we shall have lived, and pretended to live, so very much
when she comes with her eyes of rain over that river.

There will be (weary voice, impotent smile)
senile now, sterile now, dry this now that we have –
pulsing eternity, sister of silence;
the moment we now have, just as we have it now.

Yesterday, ten years ago, today, in a month –
frightful words, clichés, but what does it matter.
Drink, sleep, die – one must give stale self the slip
in one way or another...

Bridge on the Rhine

Oscar V. de L. Milosz

Melodious sweet summer-tawny downpour along the Rhine,
golden creepers drowse on balconies petalled with rust.
Music of a strange name and crying gluts the wine –
everything that has been and not been –
and goodbyes from grieving children, through the morning.

Do you look for your perished mirage in grey Rhine waters,
in the ancient flood of Rhine that finds its own quenched?
Eyes of a child queen, lips of fairies and voices in their springtime
everything that has been and not been –
and the same savor, the same and more, in this wine...

Hope? Who will keep you from hoping? Dream upon them,
yourself changed, wholly altered, the shaken years!
No more reveries, neither tomorrows nor loves for you.
Everything that has been and not been –
muse, friend, on your vast leafless solitudes.

I shall give you – but don't speak of it – the thin key
to the vault of your past, far down there in the valley
where day and night one sees snow flurrying the Rhine;
and everything that has been and not been
gleams like the towns in the tawny lakes of your wine,
in the golden lakes – the years, the years – of your dear Rhine wine.

Hidden Name

Victor Segalen

The real name gilds no portals, burnishes no deeds, nor does it feed the people their cud of resentment.

The one name cannot be conned in the halls of power, nor in gardens and grottos, but stays covered by those waters under the aquaduct arch where I slake my thirst.

Only during spells of great dryness, when winter crackles in its fixity, when the springs, at their nadir, clam themselves in ice,

when emptiness rests at the heart of the underworld and in the tunnels of the heart – blood stilled – only under the arch one can still approach does that name gather itself.

But those harsh waters melt, life gushes out, the destroying torrent comes down, rather than understanding.

from *Ode III.3, Contemplation*
Victor Segalen

All at once you are – here, then, all that you are.
    Globes exploded by decreating spheres.
    Glacial. Soothing. Divined. And diviner. Doubled
    and trinitied, centuried from the million paths.

Heaviness poured from knowledge, light as smoke.
    Permeator of the impermeable, echoes.
    Years, years! Primal babe of chaos.
    It is you who recognize the fools and heroes.

"Solang du Selbstgeworfenes fängst"
R.M. Rilke

As long as you catch what you yourself throw, it is sheer
adroitness and self-indulgent winning;
but when you suddenly become the catcher
of a ball which a woman forever playing
tosses to you, to your center, in the grace
of strict momentum, along one of those curves
sprung into the bridges that God builds:
for the first time the power to catch is a talent
not your own, but a world's. And if you really
have the strength and courage to throw it back,
no, even better, you forget strength and courage,
having already thrown... (as the year
hurls the bird, the whole migrating flock
which dying warmth flings towards a younger heat
across the ocean –) for the first time in this
adventure you rightly enter the game.
No longer do you ease up on the toss,
no longer make it harder. Out of your hands
the meteor roams and roars through all its reaches.

A cento from *Valais Quatrains*
R.M. Rilke

Like someone talking about Mother
and turning into her while talking
paths that lead nowhere
small waterfall

much shadow without doubt seeps in
threatened and redeemed
mixed from sweet evening, pure metal
wine: ardent comet

Wind taking hold of the land like the handworker
who knows, immemorially, his materials
a fine branch of terebinth
absent presence that space drank

Will the sky, in the gaze of shepherds and vintners,
held there, stay, this sky of blue wind?
Abstracted path, goats halted
poplar in place

Who, obeying summer
eternalizes it
submissive grey rose, trained vine
erased beneath these motions

Taking a long step back, the craftsman
holds his work up to the mirror of space
paths giving on nothing save the open and the season
until an appalling sun gilds them

Before you can count to ten it all changes
wind over tall stalks and the wide wave gone
unedited light beyond the range
menaced and saved

Stirred from evening sweetness the pure metal
we enter into its body
branch of terebinth that space drank
the open, the season

Ardent comet of wine
on another plane, higher
turning into her while talking
and the wide wave gone

Butterfly, sun's cousin
torn letter the lover was writing
even while the woman
was hovering at the door

Snow

Robert Walser

[The guardians of the Walser Estate, while not objecting in principle, instructed Hī-Lö that Walser's poetry is untranslatable. With Taoist fluidity he yielded. As one of these lines has it, there comes "the snow-snow-white world that leaves me powerless". Some cavities in the wall there are, then, from which no horse can drink.]

Evening on Reichenau
Martin Heidegger

["Lake silver / scatters to dark shores": a
mood captured on Walahfrid's monastery
island in lower Lake Konstanz, intended
for Heidegger's future wife, simply by
virtue of being Englished moved the
Heidegger Estate to consign it unread to
the altar fires: *carmina incinerata est*. The
ash-fringed remnant retrieved in
Frankfurt preserves the light of day's end,
fruit hanging weighty-weightless in the
hand, "in the barrens / of a great
simplicity".]

Postcard from the Engadine
(Fondly Yours, Theobald Tiger)
Kurt Tucholsky, 1926

Downstairs now at the Nietzsche house,
it's Ludwig Fulda who comes and goes.
Brilliant performance.
                    Around him, the seething
odds and ends of human beings
spat out by Berlin.
Mr Wendriner, Mrs Wendriner.
Only real dinner-jacket Berliners.
Out on their walk, the trees and grass
they have just passed through become first-class.
They snort at the waiter and raise a fuss,
missing nothing, as at the office.
The Val Fex glacier shines into the blue
while Madam declares, "Why it's simply my due –
I placed my order, paid my bill,

the magic's been painted on at my will".
Under the endless stars, they lay
them down to sleep in grey
barracks. There in the tourist hotels,
enormous snoring carressibles
loll in love's arms. How about that, arms?
Leipzig Street has sent its charms
high indeed, into bitter-sweetings...

And you, dear reader – warmest greetings!
The glacier glayshens. The rill rillows.
The sun stays switched on. The tent top billows
in the hot gusts of the high hours.
A baby is plucking bright soft flowers.
And there sits Theobald, feelingly –
  "Now who'll pluck me?"

Underworld North of Lugano

Rudolf Borchardt

Every fanatic should be crucified when he turns thirty.
  [– Goethe, Venetian Epigrams, 52]

Trekker from Italy's sideboard to the Witches' Kitchen of Germany,
  stomach turning already – now listen, *nolens volens* – don't believe
a single syllable trumpeted by headstones of the law:
  none of the megaphonic nine sets her stamp on my scroll,
nor from the heights, since coarse Germans sit among the Illuminees,
  does the stingiest laurel leaf drift over my dry bones –
but wait: I could picture Lavater dabbing at his eyes
  as he watched me in my stately robes, the Preceptor of Germany,
vanish into a contemplation which his brutal producer
  sprung a trap door under after one act. Yes! I'd like to think
that he would have seen the light, and a few others too,
  the guild's bigoted bunglers, conscience-stricken Cagliostros,
and abandoned the trivia of the lab to be hugged and soul-smooched
  into swooning over the blubbering harmonies of fledglings

swarming through Teutonic Pied Piper's Land. And that he
   would have flirted his way to being Mystery Master,
nowhere at home everywhere, courier overnighter and Clever Jack,
   and, the empire having been rigged up and given
a push, would have commanded credence right to the end among
   the gullible groundlings, going down as a wonder worker.
Not so bad! But it needs a few more ingredients, Hans Kaspar,
   than those your age gave you, God as King and Country and Our
                                                              Father
and zeal for skirts stuffed behind that starched linen collar,
   noble virtuous exalted plus a storm of progress ending in bliss.
Everything in due time, laughs the spirit of the times,
   lamely behind the times that are still greening, and so
he beats time for the times with a hoof in kiddies' shoes –
   what farce! By the time the age has its say, and Nemesis
has advanced across the field where the seeds of the age
grow stunted among the grain's tyranny, she'll have trailed
   after the triumphs and reapings, and beaten down our own
   bushelly acres, clean neat and open, until it's *tabula rasa* time.
Getting an inkling now, my dainty pathfinder? She didn't use me up,
   her man of the hour, as she did you, wrung out before her call –
I was shoved into the sweats of high climax by Asmodeus,
   who whistled through his teeth, *Do it on the sly, don't betray me,*
ease up while it's dangerous, but if that works, then do it
   like a lord swishing through the masked ball, more and more
outrageously, show them whose brat you really are,
   sweetie I wooed down the hatch to show the competition
a more frolicsome way of extracting a woman from a man.
   Go, little trump card, interrupt every act of copulation,
and, just as a magnet turns what it mates with in front
   into still another solicitor in back,
hermaphrodize me, double nature, an endless chain of hermaphrodites,
   each one a cleft that turns cleaver, a butch clinging to every queen,
until the inverted God and adored flesh in their Sabbath
   of Black Skirts show this god-forsaken world what tune to play.
Help, spirits, he's going to faint! Give this heir of Weimar
   who's crossing himself a whiff of what we are, salt of the earth,
so his virginal sensibilities, which have never heard ghouls
   cackling and kicking up their heels, will bear the brawling outcome.
Observe how faithfully I served the Master's word, *nolens volens,*
   and how everything flourished, from new Reich to scout troop,
Manlius and Maximin, and how the lineage of the revamped Germany

    found its way around Mom and Pop back to dear Auntie:
look at the evidence, dandled here in my happy arms,
    lame like the Master, who sired him on the part of me with a womb –
flashing his teeth like his dad and shiftier than the Father of Lies
    whose orders he executes through me to press nightmare upon the world.
If anyone asks where this blood-and-earth-seeking incubus comes from,
    point to me, the succubus, grand finale with double entrance,
which made it possible to bring forth Great Lord Incubus,
    or succubus of played-out eras – "As if the world were full of devils".

"Gehölz..."

Peter Huchel

Goshawk-grey
underwood
and cricket glare
of noon dessication –
the house
back from these
is built on
a vein
of water.

Water
hidden away
in sand wastes,
you gushed
into thirsting
speech,
you brought down
lightning.

At earth's
gateway
(says a voice) where
stones and roots
bar the door,
the pawed-over
bones of Job
have gone to sand,
there still stands
his bowl
of rain water.

Po-Chü-I (Pe-lo-thien)

Peter Huchel

Let me abide
in the white
wood,
steward
of wind
and cloud.
Let brightness
crease the thinking
of lone boulders.

From winter waters
climb the days,
wayward,
blind.
Masks
flayed,
they seek
freezing
the meager
scrub fire
of the fugitive
who lives
behind a wall
with his cranes and cats.

Resurrection

Peter Huchel

Snow sinking
out of fog.
Gritty street
barricaded
with the black-spiked
skeleton of a maple.
Good for a fire
but not for shoes.
The Prince is
still chasing
after Katyuscha.

"In der Verwitterung alter"

Peter Huchel

In the crumbling
of old rocks,
the secret greening
of moss.

    Evening
has his
house.
The door is
so low that
one must
bow down.

Novgorod: Coming of the Saints
Johannes Bobrowski

Now
as day breaks, light
sets out over the shores, the lake
lifts into cumulus,
around its wings birds
darken and shine,

where the wood image
floated, green graining
and the dark face
of Nicholas, a wave's
green fingers pressed it
under the river,

and came Anthony
the Stranger, a stone
wafting him over the waveless
flood, bore the man
who stepped easily
ashore: he
had seen the city,

towers and roofs,
over mountains those walls
lifting and plunging in volleys
of dark and bright fliers,
and one turret inscribed
steeply against sky.

So be it. Across my way
a cross has fallen,
sayeth Anthony, a stone –

So, fool, you also, fool,
go, fools and holy babes
over the quivering bridge.

They pass on crutches, rags
flapping their spindly arms, ancient
windbirds out of the winters.

Down the road you come shouting!
Lift this stone for me.

Assisi

Paul Celan

Umbrian night.
Umbrian night with silver of bell and olive leaf.
Umbrian night with stone that you carried here.
Umbrian night with stone.

    Mute, what welled into life, mute.
    Pour each jug its portion.

Earthen jug.
Earthen jug that hardened the potter's hand.
Earthen jug that forever inurned the hand of a shadow.

    Stone, where you keep watch, stone.
    Let the greybeast in.

Trotting beast.
Trotting through snow strewn from the nakedest hand.
Trotting before the word that tumbled in the lock.
Trotting brute who gobbles sleep from the hand.

    Gleaming, unconsoling, a gleaming.
    The dead are still begging, Francis.

On Reading a Recent Greek Poet (Buckow Elegies)
Bertolt Brecht

[Who would have guessed that one
unbudgeable piece of the Berlin Wall would read
"The Brecht Estate"? This poem, from a cycle
showing avowed Chinese influence, concerns
the Trojans and their wall, and how doom
induced them to fidget with bits of wood in their
three-ply gates, "itsy-bitsy / pieces of wood,
fussing with them". An endnote on this poem
has been left in place, as memorial to a lesser
fussing.]

Li Po (Li-Tai-Pe)
Albin Zollinger

Dreary to drag
on through China,
rain hanging
in the wheel ruts.

Drink, then!
Brother, why don't you
drink dry your lusty loping?

Wears his bones bald
trekking the land.
Pagodas rear out of forests
into the beyond,
rice pickers hang the midnight moon on their mules.

Get looped on a binge,
swill it down, your death,
let the godly
wick of wine light your way!

Mother of Kindnesses

Erika Burkart

You huddle,
honeycrone,
muffled in musk,
over shades
of the unborn
in the womb.

Hades-footed,
cranny-holy, strewn,
with the night's eyes
a trace of silvery wind
and the darting swallow's
black sickle moons
in your glance.

Twilight auguries,
whispering thickets.
Over sunken fences bends
the elderberry, angel of summer.

Between Nights

Tudor Arghezi

I planted my shovel regularly down the room.
Outside, the gusts pummeled, rain swung.

I hollowed out the room down to the ground.
Outside, pounding rain, outside, air's power.

Trench spill heaped itself at the window.
Black earth, jacketed in blue.

That mound scaled the panes.
High as the world and Jesus wept on the summit.

Digging away, the shovel shattered.
Who broke it? – the Father, on relics of rock.

I clambered back up the eras I had climbed down.
And in the room, newly naked, strode anguish.

The wish to flower on the peaks seized me.
Up there, starfire, kindling late in heaven.

Downpressings

Ion Barbu

Basilicas: shadow thickening the crowned walls –
such vigils to be mounted there
beneath nimble, evil steels:
Moscow heaven, pitchforking air.

Star carried on high in a sham
parade of prowess, with horsewhip psalms!
Explain without deviation these glories
from sunk claws, you echoing victories.

Century

Ion Barbu

To shiver out the crests of birds,
emblems slicking smooth in flight,
hooked eagles haunt the studied
radiance while you gain height.

Sickles have flashed through the waste – call out
to the wild thyme, scorched wall, to fine
ring fingers from the blank ages
beneath silver in the blinded mountain.

To the Workers in Spain
Vladimír Holan, 1936

Impossibility, red: to have one's eyes
    opened by the earth's stains!
The throbbing pulse, or the keeping of silence, or
the binding of words in sheaves, only fury explains.

Your blinding onrush, life, your cleansing force
puts out the eyes of the image by turning back –
whether it is blood poured out or the void,
does history do it, despotically swung to attack?

Join you or crush you now! is what I heard
the news thundering with agreeable speed,
when it grabbed you like a piece of fruit and bit
    down on the hard seed.

September 1938. IV
Vladimír Holan

Night of the Iliad, a night
when mountains walk, and the tribes of trees
go forth, and from a new myth
    of power great batteries
store up songs to come, and one knows
everything in them will be fulfilled,
the kind of night when jackboots make
    the globe of air tremble,
when dear life bunches its fists
to strike free of all it's been given –
the kind that only the dead command,
    no other power under heaven:
only once does such a night come...
you sense it, fresh destiny breaks in,
dimensions stay in force no more
    than a moment – no view contains it,
space lets go of its burden there.

Raptures fall from on high...for all
has become wave, now the blood hums,
   now parks grow reefs of coral,
a phantom woman altering
with the music, when the speech of speed
calls farewell on the telephone
   and the ear must let them both recede –
a man's fist grubbing swansdown
in front of a big valise, avenues
streaming from a square to shoot
   out of the throat in a scream.
The flush of love and money floods
hungrily blinking neon veins.
Plunged from the moon, time thirstily
   gulps itself from fountains.
The swell mounts, pressing its wine, dripping
vision on vision, fate in full.
Only once does such a night come
   and *only the weak* raise their wail.

May 1945

Vladimír Holan

I   I can still hear it: it was Saturday, and the fifes of the locomotives
announced to us citizens of hope in the city of hope
that we could set out for freedom from every station of the uprising.
The atmosphere, gravid for months, eager to drop its litter,
disgorged artillery and demented machine-guns
which perforated bodies
to ease them of their souls in the post office of death.
It was over quickly, and Prague, with its ripped paving,
and sand, and puddles, and toppled trees, looked as if
a new city were being founded, a borough of the abyss.

II Heroes I do not sing... their manly courage
shields their silence, our mute shame. Yet children, there were children
who for years when the sirens wailed threw their
treasures into an "air-raid bag" –
the same ones the butcher last May
drove before his tanks. Those, and the unflayed, the uncrushed,
those crying from house to house after their families
and somehow finding them, still
shriek in their sleep, "Mama, where did they take my leg?"

III And I saw a man
plugging at the German planes with a pistol...
And I saw two vans pass each other at Smichov,
one carting the corpses out of Zbraslav,
the other hauling in calves
and painted A GIFT TO PRAGUE.
Madness. But life was like that.

IV And then I know a painter: knife in hand
he stood guard over the poorhouse.
On the ninth, at daybreak, he heard pounding on the door.
Opening, he saw a dusty figure
stretch his beefy arms wide
and simply blurt out, laughing, "*Snajesch menja!*"*

V And who could forget the old codger
whose bliss it was to trot in front of the huge Russian tanks
clearing away each stone, even the smallest.

---

* "*You know me!*"

Vintage
Vítězslav Nezval, 1937

Day's end, and
from autumn mountain arbors
men and women march down,
baskets on their heads bearing the grapes,
women with vines through their hair
as strange as their lanterns,
all snake-braided,
no one is weary today
                      Lightning cascades
and nearby wait cisterns,
as also a lady in red gown,
grower whom the harvest gladdens:
jugs hang strapped overhead,
yearning choir of men, women,
a girl's breast swells with tune,
Chinese lanterns winking out
                                A meteor plunges
and back of the hills remote cities,
gleam of flaring pools
and rotting trunks over choked paths –
Listen: expansive strains
Kisses counterfeit tick-tocks
Only one in a hundred today will return home
Night crowns the restless far-off harvest with stars

Slaughterhouse
Vítězslav Nezval, 1939

The hoist hallooes
'S the way it is
Storytime creepy crawlies double
    where they do in cattle

The pulley helloes
'S the way it goes
Bemoan yourself, and trip a jig
    to the scaffold rig
The hoist hallooes
'S the way it is
To the axe in the legend came
    one Agnes by name
The wobble wheel brazens
Hope wheezes
Today to get at your throat
    the wolf steps out
Friday's the day
In the slaughterhouse hounds bay
a huskier ditty now as
    blood flows

Roman Lines

Óndra Lysohorsky, 1944

Antennae pry into space.
The atom has been quartered.
What memories, what dreams,
white Rome and tiny Athens!

Millennial shudderings
where suddenly all falls quiet.
A lone droplet plunges
to earth from impassive cloud.

Sphere – water speck – miracle,
the whole of the cosmos in it.
Elderberries on the Palatine –
below, a nightingale.

The Roman Forum rose
into the grey morning of origin –
in my vision of the ages
a mower towers haying.

Lonely tune of the fountains,
replete with distances,
but into the palace of the Caesars
strike shafts of sunlight.

The morning star pales, yet still
shines for exiled Ovid.
Remoteness enters my grasp,
my song pours with these fountains.

What burden does poetry carry
into darkness, scream, storm?
The cruellest of duties: to be
always ahead of its time.

House

Óndra Lysohorsky, 1946

Hatred makes this age, so I mean to serve
the man who goes beyond it. Look at this town:
    exquisite once, it is rubble.

A single house left standing. Rain, darkness.
A grain trucker is sheltering there –
    tomorrow he'll be far off.

That house is what I want to be:
ragged roof and crust of bread for the drivers
    who truck wheat, pushing on,

so that some day one of them, ending his run, will say:
There was a house down there, I stayed the night,
it stood in the middle of a field of ruins.

Yu-Vu Songs of the Na-khi

Boy Dawn wind shining, and the silk stars
fringeing your jacket meet my hands.
Spruce beyond roofs, quick seedlings,
we contrived no appointment,
spruce shedding to earth,
we made no arrangement,
water finds its way.
Gulley splices with runlet,
the wind gathers, arriving,
leaves loosen in acknowledgement.
Bamboo roots tangle to one clump,
massing to maturity:
the day has twelve hours,
which of them might have married us?
Paper shreds into water.
Your voice repeats the wind –
Long Tail flaps off looking
for his own singer, calling and calling.
The day waits upon us –
what are you thinking? Say it, even
as the oak ladle, balancing
the mounded barley, spills.

Girl Rushing words, meadow waters:
you are testing my youth,
the riffle purls, you wait for me to speak.
And your own speech: should I listen
as I have known others to listen –
his word into her stillness,
now you to me, yes, as you say, the two of us.
And golden rocks at the world's heart,
feel their light covering us – the mason
dares not cleave it, nor could he.
But your family is solid, with
great holdings, your father
sees in you his promise,
his esteem is your treasure....
Whatever you mean to tell me,
say it now, heap

your ladle with the dust
of this brilliance.

Boy You only, word after word:
like the bamboo knife your voice pares me.
Everything? oh yes, I have everything –
the artemisia field back of us,
the field to our left rank with sorrel,
tilling, sowing, yes, a fine future.
What do they want from me, nagging!
I don't want anything
of theirs, not one pinch.
But you, an only daughter,
your mother has given you her bronze keys,
and now she brings you a husband:
house in the hills near Dsa-du.
Do you set these aside
for our kerchief of white silk,
for the speed we shall make,
our handful of syllables?

Girl The picture of me you feed, and feed upon,
scatters seed in swamps.
Crows roost on my rooftree:
I have waited with them
long, longer than you.
Keys to my own house, yes –
but what use are they in Dsa-du,
past lakes beyond the Snow Range,
no oxen, nor cattle; and I,
I am sold into that narrow place.
Needle and silk I leave,
already I have put them
away. Mint dies on the rocks,
let us go to them, to one of the high meadows,
the three meads of Yu-vu
hugging the crags.

Boy   I have marked it with fir boughs –
a tree spreads for us in that field,
a boulder stands: I have
set our names upon it.
You can hear, under the glacier,
black water meeting white.
The silver that I hear clinking
in your sewing kit, let me
take it to Li-chiang,
the market there has silks and fine shoes,
without them I am only
a mouth speaking.

Girl   But your words trail
like ink through water, spreading:
from your brush I feel it.
You have set our names there,
let us go, then – the kerchief
and whatever else I have:
yes, to the market at Li-chiang
while the day is ours.
My home dwindling in vision,
mind clearing:
hawk's wing on the arrowshaft.
Hurry, then. The elk
wears forks of bone,
curve into curve joining;
and you will find me here.

Boy   And when I come –
the fourteenth, no, the sixteenth day,
moon not yet full, the auspices
holding (I'm yours, the cutting
lies severed) – yes,
the sixteenth, in the evening,
I shall wait above the village,
whistle three times, wait three hours.
Come to me through the leaves,
cup one in your hand
and whistle like Long Tail.

    Now, turn back home
    once more, go there slowly.

Girl I plucked the leaves as you said,
   blew on them, I have worn out three;
   but you didn't come until now!
   That house holds you
   as a jade thumb ring the bow.
   Don't look back –
   did either of us want this?
   Yet here it is,
   it is ours. Come,
   water pouring from the cup
   cannot be regathered.
   It is ours now.

Boy Rest by the fire, there is
   no buzz through this meadow.
   My reed changes like the wind.
   As I stepped across
   the threshold, my father
   stiffened in me,
   and my mother's warm sleeve –
   foot balancing on the oak doorsill
   then into air: I ran, then I
   turned back, but stopped:
   eyes blurring, spilling into the dust,
   she didn't see that, no flies
   stir their wings here – there is
   no one here but us.
   The inchworm coils forward,
   part of him spins back, arching –
   but we are here, your eyes
   are the same eyes:
   tell me, what do they say,
   what are they trying to say,
   now you must tell me.

Girl   Your foot sprang from the threshold,
your mother, the thought of her.
But she with all the others
at the pine's foot yellowing:
mushrooms die of a season, their colors
leave them, one day they are gone.
She and the others, do not
think about them,
nothing will separate us
after tomorrow, or the next day:
your foot will lift, mine fall,
that will be the way of it,
the one road, now and after.
The musk deer leaping for his cliff –
has he arrived yet?
And they will sing the Wind Ceremony
for us, nor are we the first ones –
mint over the rocks vanishing.
The evening, can't you feel it?
How can they touch us now?
Listen: at the foot of
Nine Mountains, into the pines:
stone pheasants calling.
Look neither right nor left,
the boar makes these ferns his bed.
Come, lie with me here.

Notes

Four Ancient Poems   The third incorporates bits from Ch'en Lin, Ts'ao P'i, and perhaps Cai Yong. The first line returns in "A Gross of Poems...".

January Inventory   The snake comes out of the Grossmünster's foundation legend. The transfer of power from Shun to Yü, by way of abdication near the end of the third millenium B.C., was celebrated in three poems, the first of which is rendered here. Ezra Pound's handling of the poem has been treated by John Cayley in *Agenda* for Autumn 1982-83.

Joys of the Rich   The prototype is by Li Ho.

Ditty for Mayor Fu of Freiburg im Breisgau   This city was "exempt" from air raids until 27 November 1944. The philosopher Paul Shih-yi Hsiao reflects on the behavior of the monitory duck, memorialized in bronze by the lake, in an essay which discusses his collaboration with Martin Heidegger on the translation of Lao Tzu. Heidegger's version of two lines from chapter fifteen of the *Tao Te Ching*, based on Professor Shih-yi Hsaio's rendering, underlies the last stanza here.

Rhyme Prose One   The quotation renders lines from Ion Barbu's "The Mountains".

En Avant de nos jours   Quotation from the tenth vision of Hildegard von Bingen, para. 20.

Tally Stick   "Even in / an age..." translates the first half of Saigyō's *sue no yo no*, which itself transmits a dream voice (the administrator Tankai to the poet Shunzei). The decline which is the subject of that poem is not literary but spiritual.

Sotheby Parke Bernet Renga (muted)   Hoving's extraction of the Bury St. Edmunds cross from the hands of one Ante Topic Mimara in Zurich is the subject of a memoir several times the thickness of the cross.

A Sash for Wu Yün   Wu Yün (d.778) failed the imperial examinations on Confucian topics but passed them later on Taoist ones, and spent a brief period at the court of the late T'ang emperor Hsüan-tsung. Both Wu and Li Po, whom Wu introduced to the emperor, became members of the Han-lin Academy, which, including physicians, diviners, writers, and entertainers, served the ruler directly. Both men, however, were hounded out by the court eunuch Kao Li-shih, and Wu spent the long remainder of his days as a recluse. – Both the abbot and the prior at White Cloud Monastery in Beijing, the Monte Cassino of Taoism, were murdered by their own followers in 1948, shortly before the Guomindang surrendered the city to Communist forces. Within two years, the new regime edited and reprinted the Taoist scripture *T'ai-ping ching* or Book of Great Peace, while extending no such preferment to other classics. – The end of this homage echoes a poem by Wu Yün (Kyoto no.46748), in which he approaches the immortals by climbing out of the cosmos towards blinding light.

The Death of Yuri Andropov   Alexander Solzhenitsyn reported the remark by Swiss radicals in "Our Pluralists", *Vestnik* 1983 (*Survey* 1985).

Bird Garden   "When Morning Star..." comes from the apocryphal *Liber S. Joannis*, used by the Cathars, as checked against Döllinger's edition of the fourteenth-century version. – The partridge episodes from the apocryphal *Acts of John*, including the variant from Cassian, are followed by a poem from Tung-Shan Liang-Chieh. – The snippets from Eriugena seem to come from the *Periphyseon*.

Novissima Sinica   For more on the stay in the West after World War One by Xu Zhimo, see the portrait in Jonathan Spence's *Gate of Heavenly Peace*. The opening draws on the assessment of another visitor then, Liang Qichao.

Osip Mandelshtam in the Grisons   Mandelshtam studied for two years in Paris and Heidelberg (1907-1909). Gleb Struve and Artur Lourié maintained that Mandelshtam never made his brief visit, or visits, to Italy, but Nadezhda Mandelshtam confutes them. Hī-Lö alludes to "Notre Dame", "Canzone", chapter sixteen of "The Noise of Time", and "The End of the Novel".

Seventh Moon   The ancient tale alluded to with Turnip and Nīladhi, the *Maudgalyayana*, was recovered among scrolls at the caves of Tun-huang.

Colgan over Cogitosus, or Kan Pao Prosimetrics   Colgan and Cogitosus were both seventh-century biographers of St. Brigit. Colgan included the pagan background which Cogitosus suppressed. Kan Pao, in the words of Kenneth DeWoskin, "collected material unsuitable for inclusion in the dynastic history, even though he was the official compiler of that record. He made these 'left-overs' (*yü-shih*) into his *In Search of the Supernatural*, acknowledging his anxiety that such materials were otherwise in danger of being lost, and there might be something of value to be found in them" (*Doctors, Diviners, and Magicians of Ancient China*).

A Gross of Poems Linked in the Mixed Manner Hĭ-Lö's notes account for the two groups of inset poems along archaic lines: the whole is a cauldron or *t'ing* with flaws in the rim to permit the spirits free passage. (The first group, beginning at 50A, alludes not only to the ancient "long wall caves" poem but also to strikes that were brutally suppressed during construction of the alpine tunnels.) – No.35: line two renders part of Wu Wenying's "To the Tune of *Mulankua man*". – Nos.64-65: the Basel exhibit by Joseph Buys. – No.120: this house became a hotel. – No.133: an early professor of Medicine at Zurich, Dr Moleschott proposed that "one is what one eats".

The Cells at Tun-huang The cave-like cells at this Buddhist desert monastery were built over several hundred years. The fresco showing episodes from the ancient tale of the golden stag, in the *Ruru-Jataka*, was painted ca. 500 A.D.

Single Seal Quodlibets... Western Palace Rhapsodies These seven poems stem from Hĭ-Lö's notes on Bernhard Karlgren's revision of his *Grammatica Serica*. Karlgren's scholarship, offering compendia of archaic inscriptions and the traditions of their interpretation, seems to have supplied Hĭ-Lö with staging-points for westward raids from eastern outposts still shrouded in mist.

"Writing alters..." Liu Xie's maturity coincided, in the early sixth century, with a peak phase of literary innovation. His position in debates between ancients and moderns is represented here. "Writing" is *wen*, "patterns" of every kind, from macrocosmic to psychological; and with his braided rope he may be recalling the fact that in the transition from prehistory writing replaced "government by knotted ropes".

Poem on Divine Providence This long poem was attributed by Migne in the *Patrologia Latina* to St. Prosper of Aquitaine. The misattribution puts one in mind of context, for Prosper compiled an anthology of Augustine's work, whose readers would have found that the calamities described as remote in *The City of God* were on their own backs. Orientius was a Pelagian Christian. He brought his experience as prisoner of war into the poem, alongside a confidence in spiritual survival which Hī-Lö's selections do not translate.

My Country Weeps: 1636   "Das Rathaus liegt im Graus...": *Graus* may double for both rubble and fear. – Hī-Lö's "conduits of blood": Shakespeare.

Venus de Milo, Gottfried Keller   Compare Flaubert, *Un Coeur simple*: "La pendule, au milieu, représentait un temple de Vesta".

"*Quand elle viendra...*" and *Bridge on the Rhine*   These two poems from Milosz's work before its turning point, while melancholy, are not without contrapuntal ties to Milosz's later affirmations. The second line of the fourth stanza in "When she comes..." duplicates, in Milosz's French, the rhythm of Mallarmé's "le vierge, le vivace, et le bel aujourd'hui". Professor Mortimer Guiney attuned Hī-Lö's ear to this homage, whose rhythm Hī-Lö then carried into his own version of the line.

Underworld North of Lugano, Rudolf Borchardt   Unpublished during Borchardt's lifetime; written in Italy in 1937 when he was sixty and already resident there since the 'twenties. From a Königsberg Protestant family of Jewish origin, Borchardt was hostile to much in the modern German temper. He affiliated himself with Stefan George, defending George in essays from 1909 through 1928. The title originally named Locarno (near which George is buried, having fled to Switzerland one year before his death in 1934), but Lugano seems, as Borchardt's editors suggest, to separate German and Italian cultural spheres more exactly – and Borchardt's translations of Dante, the troubadors, and Greek lyric bear out his dedication to a Mediterranean focus. Stefan George's major poems anticipate the German catastrophe; but his circle included Alfred Schuler, the anti-Semite who excavated the swastika from Bachofen and gave it to Hitler. The fierce backlash from Borchardt against his former master George stems, after the Nazi consolidation of power, in part from George's earlier association with Schuler (although George had repudiated him). The homosexual and bisexual practices of members of George's circle stand, it seems, behind the grotesque masquerade choreographed here by Asmodeus. (Schuler believed himself to be a reincarnated Roman Aryan, and at a Munich Mardi Gras dressed as the Magna Mater, next to George's Julius Caesar. The Indo-European Great Mother in Bachofen lends Schuler the swastika, and so here may explain the "Auntie" behind a "revamped" German lineage.) "Manlius and Maximin" name, respectively, a homosexual prostitute in one of George's

Roman poems, and George's homosexual lover, dead at sixteen. The "scout troop" alludes, then, to the George circle, as well as to Nazi youth organizations. "The new Reich" also titles one of George's volumes, from 1928. The animadvertive digression to Johann Kaspar Lavater, Zurich pastor and pioneer psychologist (his meteoric phase of genius here becomes a "one-act" performance), sets up a parallel master-disciple relation, with parallel defection, for the young Goethe made pilgrimages to Lavater but later mocked his Swiss piety (the unattributed epigraph from the *Venetian Epigrams* satirizes Lavater). This tortuous monologue draws, then, upon Borchardt's own role vis-à-vis his master to graph schisms in the German spirit which he found diagnostic. The ironic allusion to "Preceptor of Germany" – the title awarded to the early reformer Melanchthon – Borchardt aims at himself, with a force that equals the backlash, however unfair, against George. Were the targets merely personal, then neither the intellectual responsibility nor the demonism would concern a whole people. The last hemistich implies an exorcism; it comes from that verse in Luther's *Ein feste Burg* which ends, "ein Wörtlein kann ihn fällen".

Assisi   Inscribed here within public allusions to St Francis is a discreet elegy for Celan's first son Franz.

On Reading a Recent Greek Poet, Bertolt Brecht   The Greek poet is Kavafis, whose "Trojans" (1905) Brecht had seen in 1953 in Helmut von den Steinen's translation, which he echoes at two points. In June came the uprisings by workers in Berlin and other cities of the DDR. The *Buckow Elegies* were drafted quickly that summer; though Brecht publically sided with Ulbricht and the regime, the poems do not. Stalinism seems to meet with a Taoist objection in "Steel", where metal-shackled scaffolding collapses in a dream-storm while "anything made of wood / yielded and endured". Though it is not unfair to see Brecht craftily maintaining, in Ronald Gray's words a "self-preserving, chameleon attitude" side by side with an Austrian passport, the reflective part of the chameleon writes these poems, one model for which, as Brecht indicated, was Chinese poetry.

Between Nights...House   Only Tudor Arghezi, among the East European writers selected by Hï-Lö, lived as an exile in Switzerland. The two poems by Óndra Łysohorsky were first composed in German. Verses from the Czech of Holan and Nezval occasionally have benefitted from the work of other translators, namely Franz Fühmann, Pierre Garnier, Uwe Grüning, Ludvik Kundera, Luc-André Marcel, and Vilém Reich-mann. – In Vítězslav Nezval's "Vintage", the woman in red gown, given certain other features of the poem, alludes to the Apocalyptic Woman in St John's vision.

Yu-Vu Songs of the Na-khi   Such folksongs by shepherds, about suicide pacts among lovers from this Tibetan and southwestern-Chinese tribe, were drawn on briefly by Ezra Pound in Canto CX. The particular ballad-like cycle rendered here, with formulaic repetition removed, was first translated by the scholar to whom we owe our knowledge of this people, Joseph Rock ("The Romance of Ka-Mä-Gyu-Mi-Gkyi: a Na-khi Tribal Love Story", *Bulletin de l'École Française de l'Extrème Orient* XXXIX, 1939). Imported Chinese marriage customs made these pacts common, and the Na-khi developed a ceremony for the propitiation of spirits lost in suicide, the "sway of the wind ceremony". The lovers are believed to join the mountain winds of the high groves and meadows in which they carry out *yu-vu*. The songs are typically improvised by young shepherds on triple-reed Jew's harps, in lines of five syllables sung in syncopated rhythm.